Reclaiming
Derelict Land

J. R. OXENHAM

FABER AND FABER LTD
24 Russell Square
London

First published in mcmlxvi
by Faber and Faber Limited
24 Russell Square London WC1
Printed in Great Britain by
Latimer Trend & Co Ltd Plymouth

Contents

5

Contents

clay, sand and other mineral spoilheaps—Cement, pottery, glass and chemical wastes—Ash and clinker tips—Slag heaps—Hill and dale formations

Contents

LIST OF TABLES

LIST OF DIAGRAMS

Contents

Illustrations

Illustrations

16. Peterborough brickworks showing flooded marlholes at Fletton, 1948

17. Peterborough brickworks. Land reclamation scheme in progress during 1963, using pulverized fuel ash for filling

between pages 112 and 113

18. Euclid. T.C. 12. Crawler tractor with twin engines developing 425 h.p. fitted with cable-operated bulldozer. Ironstone workings, Corby, Northamptonshire

19. Challenger crawler tractor fitted with angledozer

20. Euclid. T.C. 14. All wheel drive motor scraper. Capacity 14 cubic yards (struck) to 20 cubic yards (heaped). Twin diesel engines (front and rear), each of 148 h.p.

21. R. G. Le Tourneau self-loading electric digger. Powered by two 475 h.p. diesel engines coupled to A.C. and D.C. generators with electric motors at all points of power application, including a D.C. motor in each wheel. Capable of self-loading at the rate of one ton per second

22. Aveling-Barford. 99H. motor grader with 15 h.p. diesel engine. Independent drive and steering to each wheel. Hydraulic blade manipulation allows for a banking angle up to 90 deg.

23. The elevating-grader

24. R. G. Le Tourneau rubber-tyred electric excavator-loader with articulated steering. Bucket capacity from 16 to 24 cubic yards

25. N.C.K.—Rapier. Face shovel with $3\frac{1}{2}$ cubic yard bucket. For heavy duty digging and loading

26. N.C.K.—Rapier. Dragline with 60-foot boom and $1\frac{3}{4}$ cubic yard bucket

27. A small skimmer excavator

28. Euclid. R. 45. Rear dump lorry. Payload 45 tons. Capacity 30 cubic yards (struck) to 36 cubic yards (heaped). 530 h.p. diesel engine. Twin three-stage double acting hoist jacks for tipping

29. Twin tyne heavy duty ripper fitted to rear of wheeled tractor

30. Sheepsfoot Vibroll. Weighs $5\frac{1}{4}$ tons and is usually tractor hauled. A 52 h.p. diesel engine, mounted at the rear, operates the Vibrator gear, housed within the roll

31. A rotavator that can be attached to any three-point linkage tractor up to 60 h.p. It gives a depth of cut up to 8 inches and a tillage width of 70 inches

Illustrations

32. Tree transplanting Machine. The scoop or shovel-blade has dug out the root ball and the mature tree has been lifted and is being transported to its new location. A pioneering experiment by the National Coal Board at Shortwood Opencast site, Trowell, Nottinghamshire

33. Shale planer in one of the deep Lower Oxford claypits at King's Dyke near Whittlesea

between pages 152 and 153

34. Derelict land reclaimed to provide sites for new industries at Tonypandy, Glamorganshire

35. Former gravel pits at Water Orton, Warwickshire, filled with pulverized fuel ash from Hams Hall electricity generating station and restored to agriculture

36. Derelict land restored to agriculture at Coton Farm, Nether Whiteacre, Warwickshire. Filling operations in progress

37. First barley crop being harvested

38. Hydraulic seeding—Spraying on seed mixture and fertilizers

39. Hydraulic seeding—Applying the mulch of chopped straw and bituminous emulsion

40. Wilmington, Co. Durham, dominated by colliery spoilheap

41. Colliery spoilheap at Croxdale near Durham before planting in 1956. Note River Wear at base of spoilheap and main line railway viaduct on left

42. Croxdale spoilheap in 1965 with trees well established. Main line viaduct as reference point

between pages 184 and 185

43. Trees planted on spoilheap at Littleburn near Durham becoming established

44 (a and b). A good example of the screening of industrial plant

45. Well screened gravel workings showing the tree screen in background and an island left for wildfowl in foreground

46. Chasewater, reclaimed as a water sports area. The adjoining recreational area was filled and levelled with pulverized fuel ash from the Rugeley electricity generating station

47. An old gravel pit at Dorchester-on-Thames, Oxfordshire, which has received amenity treatment

48. Mining subsidence at Kimblesworth, Co. Durham. Houses in foreground demolished. Houses in background shored up

11

ACKNOWLEDGEMENTS

The courtesy of the following, in allowing photographs to be published is gratefully acknowledged: J. R. Atkinson, Esq.— County Planning Officer, Durham; Aveling-Barford Limited; J. A. Barratt, Esq.—County Planning Officer, Staffordshire; Blackwood Hodge; J. J. Brooks, Esq.—County Planning Officer, Warwickshire; Central Electricity Generating Board, Midlands Region; Central Office of Information; Hydraumatic Seeding Limited; Howard Rotavator Co. Ltd.; P. G. Laws, Esq.—County Planning Officer, Bedfordshire; National Coal Board; N.C.K.-Rapier Ltd.; Jack Olding and Co. Ltd.; Royal Air Force; Sand and Gravel Association; Stothert and Pitt, Ltd.; T. W. Ward, Ltd.

Foreword

by Sir HERBERT J. MANZONI, C.B.E., D.Sc.

Past President of the Institution of Civil Engineers
Past President of the Institution of Municipal Engineers

The evils of derelict land and the urgent need for its reclamation have provided themes for many lectures and publications during the last twenty years, but few have shown how to tackle the unusual and varied problems involved and none has dealt comprehensively with the actual mechanics of the task. To follow up the propaganda, there is need for a textbook, collating the experience to date and dealing with the design of reclamation schemes and the practical problems that arise in the field. John Oxenham has written just such a textbook for civil and municipal engineers, landscape architects and planners faced with the detailed design of reclamation projects and it should be of immense value also to public works contractors, manufacturers, owners and operators of earth-moving equipment, as well as to all industrialists and mineral operators who may be under an obligation to restore land in accordance with the conditions of a planning consent. Members and officials of Local Authorities and Local Planning Authorities that have derelict areas within their boundaries should find the book invaluable and at the same time, covering the wide field and many disciplines that it does, it should be invaluable also as a textbook in the Universities, Colleges of Advanced Technology, Schools and Training Centres.

As a Royal Engineer during the 1939–1945 war, the author

13

obtained a great deal of experience in the employment of heavy mechanical equipment for the construction of airfields, aerodromes and roads throughout the Middle East. Later in Italy, as officer in charge of timber production from the Calabrian forests, he obtained an insight into the best Italian forestry practice, which is probably the oldest and most advanced in the world.

After the war was over, he came to Birmingham as Regional Planning Officer for the Ministry of Town and Country Planning and his experience was quickly put to good account in advising Local Authorities how to tackle land reclamation problems, especially during the post-war housing campaign. In close co-operation with officers of the Ministry of Agriculture, a large number of housing and development projects were steered from virgin land to sites that needed reclamation in the Black Country, the Potteries and in Coalbrookdale. During the last twenty years, the author has been involved in the reclamation of some twelve thousand acres throughout the country and it is clear that this book deals with most of the problems which emerged and upon which his advice was sought.

Within his profession, the author is quite well known and requires little introduction, having served on both the Council of the Institution of Municipal Engineers and the Council of the Town Planning Institute. In 1932 the Institution published his *Handbook of Municipal Engineering Law* for the benefit of the Widows and Orphans Benevolent Fund. Since the early nineteen thirties, he has made notable contributions to professional research and discussions of current problems in various theses and papers for which he has been awarded the Richard Pickering Gold Medal (1932); the Public Works Congress Silver Medal (1939) and Bronze Medals (1939 and 1952); Bronze Medals of the Institution of Municipal Engineers (1940 and 1948) and the Owens Prize of the Royal Society of Health (1954).

Land conservation and environment improvement are two of the most important functions of physical planning and a vital component of both is the restoration of damaged land to usefulness and fertility. These are objectives which merit universal

Foreword

approval and support. This book shows how such work can be done and it comes at a time when many Local Authorities, new to reclamation tasks, will be embarking upon clearance programmes. On all sides, large schemes are being undertaken like the Lea Valley project of the Civic Trust; the Tyneside improvement proposals; landscaping of the Yorkshire motorways; the Lower Swansea Valley rehabilitation scheme and the Lothians Regional plan for environmental improvement. There is an ever-pressing demand for land in this small island of ours, and its increasing population will force us to reclaim and use again every acre that can be made productive or amenable to our needs. I consider this book to be most timely and very valuable.

Birmingham
February 1966

Preface

by LORD HOLFORD

Past president of the Royal Institute of British Architects.
Past President of the Town Planning Institute.
Trustee of the Institute of Landscape Architects.

It is possible for the Englishman to avoid art and be deaf to music, but he is very unlikely to ignore landscape. He is sensitive to it as something which he not only sees with his eyes but helps to create with his hands. It appeals to his practical as well as his poetic sense.

John Oxenham is one of these. He has an eye for country, in the tradition of Izaac Walton or Gilbert White of Selborne. His field of action has been very different from theirs (as Sir Herbert Manzoni has briefly mentioned in his foreword to this book). But he has the same ability to observe detail, the same respect for facts, and the same capacity for recognizing the natural history and the natural philosophy behind the facts. Such men have much of value to hand on to their successors, especially when their observation has been accurate and their experience has been systematically recorded. John Oxenham has been additionally generous in writing this book, for he has donated in advance to the Institute of Landscape Architects all his author's fees, so as to inaugurate a fund for '. . . the encouragement of any work which promotes an improvement in the human environment'.

This gesture, too, has its practical as well as its idealistic side

Preface

as Kipling wrote: 'Our England is a garden, and such gardens are not made by singing: "Oh, how beautiful!" and sitting in the shade . . .'.

So John Oxenham gets down at once to the job of reclamation by analysing types and causes, listing the legal and financial means to cope with the problem, specifying the mechanical equipment available, and discussing techniques such as those for soil-conditioning, pioneer vegetation, and tree planting. His whole contribution to the subject is remedial and positive; this alone should commend it to the creative instincts of architects, engineers, landscape designers and planners, as well as those directly concerned with conservation. But it is also interesting to read, as well as useful to refer to.

Our artificial and our natural environments are interdependent, and will become increasingly so as time goes on and populations grow. John Oxenham shows us how to recognize the assaults that Man makes on Nature and the growing potential that we have for reversing the process by reclaiming land that has, for any reason, become derelict.

His book is a significant contribution to what might be called Landscape Information, and also to the Institute which becomes the recipient of his gift.

London
March 1966

Part One

INTRODUCTORY

CHAPTER 1

The Nature of Dereliction

In a social sense the term 'derelict land' is commonly used to describe land which is uncared for or which has been damaged by some use or process and then neglected. In the legal sense, the term refers to land which has been relinquished or abandoned by its owner. In an agricultural context the term can include any large areas of land which are completely or comparatively unproductive such as, on the one hand—sand-dunes, saltings, marshes or land liable to flooding and on the other hand—poor quality moorland, marginal land or hill country which is relatively inaccessible. From a landscape standpoint the term is applied to land which has become unsightly and derelict through human activities and industrial operations. As such there can be infinite variety in its appearance. The surface can be fairly level but barren of vegetation or it may be pitted with deep furrows, excavations and marlholes, or disfigured with monstrous spoilheaps, ridges and mounds like a lunar landscape. The surface covering can vary from coarse grass or rough scrub to bare rock, slag, slate, shraff, chemical wastes or just infertile subsoil or yet again, the land may be covered with water or it may be subject to flooding or liable to subsidence.

The common conception of derelict land refers to a neglected appearance which is such as to give offence to the eye. This conception is not really concerned with the legal accident of ownership; it refers not to land in which the owner has relinquished his rights of ownership but to land in which he appears to have abandoned all care for its appearance. Such is the nature of the industrial dereliction with which we will be concerned, and it may be defined as land which has been damaged by extractive or other industrial processes, which in its existing state is unsightly and incapable of reasonably beneficial use and which is likely to remain so, unless subjected to special reclamation treatment.

Man may be justified in exploiting the world's natural resources for his benefit, comfort and profit. It may be defensible that he should enjoy the mineral wealth of the universe to the utmost limits to which it can be won by him, trusting that succeeding generations will find alternative raw materials or invent methods for more intensive working. For instance, in many areas, gravel reserves are being exhausted at a prodigal rate with the consolation that our successors will probably discover other constructional materials or devise new methods of building. The coal resources of the world that accumulated throughout untold ages have been feverishly exploited by the comparatively few generations that have mined them, nevertheless it seems likely that posterity will have ample alternative sources of energy. But even if man is justified in extracting and consuming the natural wealth, he cannot be entitled to leave the land wasted and despoiled. Succeeding generations will want the use of it and whatever it costs, it should at least be handed on, in as fertile, sightly and useful a state as can be achieved.

THE OPERATION OF PLANNING CONTROL

The repair of damaged sites is one of the functions of planning control in order to ensure that the national asset, which land represents, is conserved, redeveloped and put to a new use. Planning control was first fully applied under the Town and Country Planning Act 1947 which enables conditions to be attached to permissions for development. These conditions apply not only to the form of development permitted but also to the ultimate state of the land after development ceases. The planning conditions imposed, which are backed by enforcement powers, are becoming increasingly effective by ensuring that sites are restored or at least left in a reasonably tidy condition after their development or exploitation has been completed, and this applies particularly to the dereliction which results from mineral working. Before new mineral workings can commence, permission has to be obtained from the local planning authority and where this is granted, it is normally subject to conditions that provide for the land surface, either to be reinstated or landscaped and rendered presentable upon abandonment of the workings.

However, there is a large legacy of dereliction from the past and occasionally the enforcement of planning controls proves to be impracticable for various reasons, and these circumstances leave areas which will form the hardcore of the problem in the future. A great deal of pioneering reclamation work has been done upon such areas by many Local Authorities, and the Ministry of Housing and Local Government has encouraged the promotion of reclamation schemes in circulars and memoranda as well as by the issue of advisory brochures. For a number of years, the policy has been to expedite clearance of these dead lands and to give them new life by redevelopment. To this end the development plans of all local planning authorities have been utilized to secure a programmed solution to the problem.

What causes dereliction?

The extraction of minerals, and the disposal of waste products from mineral workings and manufacturing industry, have been the main causes of industrial dereliction. Basically, the majority of manufacturing processes are conversions of natural or raw materials into fabrications and synthesized products. This involves a continuous demand upon the various elemental substances and these have to be won from the earth. This winning of mineral wealth may be accomplished by mining, quarrying or open cast working, and each of these processes gives rise to a different type of dereliction. Furthermore, the form of dereliction and its effect upon the landscape generally varies from one industry to another, and frequently within the same industry it may vary between one district and another as a result of local working conditions or customs or owing to the different stratification of the minerals.

Thus it is that mining almost always gives rise to subsidence which in some circumstances may cause flashes or craters, and in this country, mining is invariably accompanied by tips and spoilheaps of variant shape and size. Quarrying generally scars or pockets a hillside, or it may crumble through a ridge, or it may take the form of a deep depression below surface level descending in giant steps. Open cast working frequently results in the familiar 'hill and dale' formation, or it may create deep marlholes partly filled with water, or extensive sand, gravel or chalk pits. Most mineral workings leave a depression of one kind or another unless the extractions and reinstatement are planned and programmed together, as is customary, in winning sand for glass manufacture or unless stowage or backfilling is undertaken. The surface depressions resulting from deep coalmining and brine pumping (in the winning of salt) are often waterlogged or flooded over large parts of the undermined area owing to disruption of the natural drainage by subsidence and these depressions are commonly known as 'flashes' or 'meres'.

When the manufacturing or extractive industries produce by-products or wastes which are of little or no commercial value, these wastes are generally tipped into spoilheaps which vary widely in size from industry to industry according to the volume of production and the proportion of waste. Some industries produce eight times as much waste as they do of finished product. The shape of the spoilheaps usually depends upon the method of tipping which is employed. The most common forms are the high, conical tip, the high or low ridge tip or hogsback and the low plateau tip. Throughout the country there are created in all forms and sizes those colliery shale tips; quarry stone waste heaps; iron and steel slag banks; ash, cinder and clinker mounds; metallic dross heaps; chemical waste mounds; shraff, saggers and pottery waste tips, sand and clay mounds that are characteristic and prominent features of the local land-

Plate 1. Sand and Gravel Workings. General view of a processing plant in Sussex

Plate 2. Excavating and loading gravel into barges from a wet pit

Plate 3. Penrhyn Slate Quarries showing some of the twenty-two galleries of this amphitheatre in the Welsh mountains

Plate 4. Mineral workings on Lee Moor, Devon

Plate 5. A china clay mine near St. Austell, Cornwall

scapes. So much so, that certain parts of the country are permanently associated with one or more of these features—the form of the dereliction conveys the image of the locality and of its industry. Unfortunately this impression is generally an unpleasant one.

To add still greater variety to the problems of dereliction, large industrial sites are occasionally closed down and abandoned as trade and manufacturing demands fluctuate, raw materials become exhausted or more favourable locations are found. These abandoned industrial sites commonly include steelworks and blast furnaces; colliery buildings with winding gear, deep shafts, waggon sidings and spoilheaps; quarry buildings and obsolete stone-crushing plant; brickyards with kilns, high chimneys and marlholes; heavy engineering and chemical works with massive plant foundations and associated tanks, filters and lagoons. Then there are the long narrow stretches of discarded railways and disused canals which like abandoned airfields are pertinent to our discussion. An outstanding example of the wide variety and diverse interests involved in large abandoned industrial sites is to be seen at Landore in the lower Swansea valley (*vide* page 186). The volume of work involved can be immense, as was instanced at Tinsley Park, Sheffield (*vide* page 118). The smaller quarries, brickyards and miscellaneous engineering works generally involve sites of only five to ten acres and there are examples of these in all parts of the country. But when the largest quarries, steelworks, collieries and manufactories are abandoned they can leave some hundreds of acres derelict in each site.

The Production of Surface Minerals

Britain is a manufacturing country with a rich variety of minerals within small compass. Since the commencement of the industrial revolution there has been an enormous demand for raw materials. As population has increased, more and more pressure has been generated to satisfy the rapidly expanding industrial and constructional requirements. The minerals production graph has been rising steadily since the turn of the century.

All mineral extraction leaves its mark on the land, but by their nature, surface mineral workings are the most obtrusive, particularly when the mineral deposits are shallow and in heavy demand, for this results in the stripping of extensive areas. There is a large group of minerals within this category including gravel, sand, clay, limestone, chalk, sandstone, ironstone, the igneous rocks and open cast coal. Most of these have the characteristics of wide distribution, occurrence as outcrops or surface deposits and high annual output which is reviewed below to give an appreciation of the magnitude of the problem.

The latest figures giving the output of **sand and gravel** (including chert, flint, moulding sand and silica sand) show that it is now running at a rate exceeding 84 million tons per year and it has been conservatively estimated that this involves a surface consumption of at least 3,000 acres each year. Most of these deposits are shallow and have only a thin overburden, but there

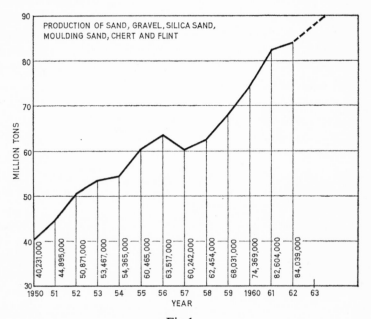

Fig 1

are some deep gravel pits in the North of England and in the Midlands. In every part of the country many terrace, alluvial and glacial gravels are worked below the permanent water table and when these are worked out they leave extensive lagoons. (See Plates 1 and 2.) However, the majority of mineral workings are dry and when they cease, depressions and hollows are left, having rough stony surfaces which can remain stark and infertile for a long period unless they receive restoration treatment.

Limestone, chalk, igneous rocks, sandstone and slate are in constant demand for all forms of building and constructional work including the manufacture of cement and lime and the provision of road metalling. These materials occur in comparatively thick beds and are normally won by excavating below ground level or by quarrying into a hillside. Their combined output is of the order of 81 million tons per year and it has been estimated that these workings consume some 800 acres annually. Where working takes the form of an excavation it is usually deep, stepped and frequently flooded. When the working makes a re-entrant in a hillside, the rough stony face can cut across the landscape like an open gash. (See Plate 3). Where it eats away

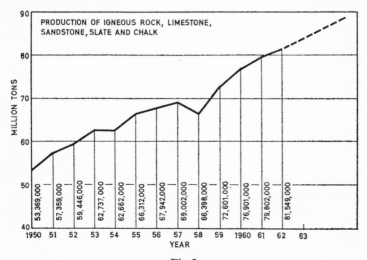

Fig 2

27

a crest or gnaws through a ridge it invariably spoils the natural profile. Quarries also produce waste and this is normally formed into conical heaps in the vicinity of the quarry but clear of the quarry floor. The amount of waste produced varies widely—about 90 per cent of the slate quarried is tipped to waste, on the other hand the waste from limestone quarries may be less than 3 per cent. Much depends upon the physical properties of the stone, the scope for by-products and the demand for filling in the locality.

Clay is won from many geological formations and the term includes the cement shales, fireclay, brick clay, ball clay, china clay, etc. (See Plate 4.) The total annual output is of the order of 36 million tons and at least 400 acres are taken for new workings each year. The beds are generally thick and extensive, so the workings take the form of deep marl holes in Staffordshire and deep china claypits in Cornwall or the wide expanse of the Fletton brickfields in Bedfordshire and at Peterborough. The deeper excavations are frequently flooded to an appreciable depth, on the other hand the brick-clay workings of eastern and

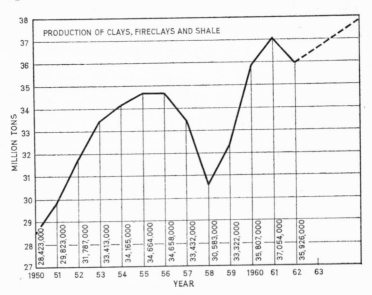

Fig 3

southern England as well as the limestone shales used for the manufacture of cement, usually have a thin bed and a thin cover of overburden which result in shallow but extensive excavations. Fireclays and pottery clays are frequently mined by driving adits from the bottom of a marlhole or claypit, in which case, the excavations cannot be filled or reclaimed until all mining ceases. In the coalfields, marlholes can frequently be found adjoining spoilheaps and a similar circumstance obtains in Cornwall where the china clay pits are accompanied by huge waste heaps of white quartz sand. A further item of dereliction occurs in china clay areas when the mica screens and slurry dams form lagoons which can sterilize appreciable areas of land. (See Plate 5.)

Ironstone is being won at a rate of about 16 million tons per annum and it has been estimated that some 450 acres of land are consumed each year. In Oxfordshire, Warwickshire, Leicestershire and South Lincolnshire the mineral occurs as a relatively thin bed with a thin cover of overburden and in these districts the workings are comparatively shallow and have a dry floor. But in Northamptonshire and North Lincolnshire there is a thick overburden of limestone which creates a dereliction in the form of a massive 'hill and dale' of limestone blocks that is much more difficult to restore. However, under the Town and Country Planning Act 1947 and since the Ironstone Restoration Fund was established under the Mineral Workings Act of 1951, practically all worked ironstone land in the Midlands has been or is being restored and the cost of restoration work is largely borne as a charge upon the industry.

Coal is also won by open cast working. From a peak of 14·3 million tons in 1958, production has fallen in more recent years to 7·6 million tons. For a long period these workings involved the annual disturbance of some 7,000 acres of land. As the coal is generally found in seams which vary from two feet to six feet in thickness, beneath a thick overburden, the resulting dereliction is of the 'hill and dale' type. But all this dereliction is only temporary because complete restoration of the land surface to agriculture by levelling, grading, re-draining and cultivation is

TABLE I. Annual Production of Minerals since 1950

(Thousand Tons)

	1950	1951	1952	1953	1954	1955	1956	1957	1958	1959	1960	1961	1962
Chert and Flint	240	234	175	86	124	137	182	169	152	98	157	172	142
Moulding Sand	689	671	720	739	755	798	759	760	735	768	836	723	700
Gravel and Sand (including silica sand)	39,302	43,990	49,976	52,642	53,486	59,530	62,576	59,313	61,567	67,165	73,376	81,709	83,197
Total	40,231	44,895	50,871	53,467	54,365	60,465	63,517	60,242	62,454	68,031	74,369	82,604	84,039
China Clay	735	909	790	809	972	1,144	1,196	1,224	1,213	1,312	1,638	1,718	1,464
Potters Clay and Ball Clay	379	393	386	343	360	413	428	460	449	446	522	535	549
Clay, Shale, Diatomite, etc.	23,585	24,569	26,420	28,133	28,954	29,317	29,397	28,404	25,999	27,781	30,819	32,150	31,984
Fireclay	2,272	2,540	2,787	2,742	2,523	2,454	2,583	2,442	2,180	2,075	2,159	2,183	1,929
Oil Shale	1,452	1,412	1,404	1,386	1,356	1,336	1,054	902	742	708	669	468	
Total	28,423	29,823	31,787	33,413	34,165	34,664	34,658	33,432	30,583	32,322	35,807	37,054	35,926
Chalk	12,930	13,292	14,294	15,346	15,624	16,539	16,755	16,220	14,108	15,363	15,505	15,498	17,898
Igneous Rock	11,243	12,397	12,693	12,912	13,217	13,958	14,333	14,167	14,388	15,655	16,265	17,393	17,679
Limestone	24,964	27,371	27,945	29,814	29,356	31,242	32,285	33,845	33,081	37,238	40,079	41,912	40,742
Sandstone	4,084	4,137	4,371	4,526	4,320	4,435	4,443	4,639	4,710	4,251	4,959	4,902	5,137
Slate	148	162	143	139	145	138	126	131	111	94	93	97	93
Total	53,369	57,359	59,446	62,737	62,662	66,312	67,942	69,002	66,398	72,601	76,901	79,802	81,549
Deep Mined Coal	204,140	211,880	214,320	212,500	213,990	210,190	209,920	210,060	201,470	195,280	186,050	181,900	190,100
Open Cast Coal	12,190	11,010	12,170	11,710	10,100	11,370	12,080	13,570	14,350	10,830	7,550	8,600	7,300
Total	216,330	222,890	226,490	224,210	224,090	221,560	222,000	223,630	215,820	206,110	193,600	190,500	197,400
Ironstone	12,271	13,539	15,560	15,965	15,353	15,859	15,936	16,568	14,613	14,637	16,934	16,401	15,232

Source: Ministry of Power and Abstract of Statistics, Central Statistical Office.

30

undertaken as a routine charge upon the industry. (See Plate 6.)

The total production of surface minerals is now running at about 220 million tons per year. It has been estimated that of this total, some 70 million tons are won above ground level and 150 million tons are excavated. Of the excavations it is probable that where dry pits are involved about one-third should be capable of restoration at a lower level and about two-thirds may need filling. In the case of wet excavations—many of these lend themselves for conversion into water recreation areas.

Where is this Derelict Land?

Dereliction is ubiquitous; it can be found in the depths of the countryside as well as in the midst of urban communities; it can afflict a small remote rural district as much as a large county borough. However, there is a marked concentration in districts associated with the emergence of the coal, iron, steel and chemical industries, particularly where those industries have subsequently declined and removed to newer industrial districts.

As might be expected there are outstanding concentrations of dereliction associated with general urban blight within industrial areas like Camborne-Redruth (2,635 acres), Merthyr Tydfil (1,827 acres), Stoke-on-Trent (1,634 acres), Newcastle under Lyme (1,067 acres), St. Austell (1,020 acres) and Ebbw Vale (1,003 acres) but the surprisingly large amount of 56,000 acres can be found scattered over rural districts and in the heart of the country.

The first estimate of the total amount of dereliction in England and Wales was made in a paper presented by the author to the Institution of Municipal Engineers in 1948.

This was a conservative estimate of 120,000 acres, but even so the extent of dereliction that it revealed was larger than had generally been thought to exist. This led to some further discussion at the Public Works Congress in 1952 and a Working Party was set up in 1954, within the Ministry of Housing and Local Government, to examine and report upon the problems of derelict land. The Working Party issued a questionnaire to local planning authorities and the returns showed that 126,700 acres were derelict. Included in this total were 51,000 acres of spoil-heaps, 53,000 acres of excavations and 23,000 acres of other forms of dereliction. A summary of these returns was published by the Ministry on page 2 of Technical Memorandum No. 7 which was circulated to local planning authorities.

In the Northern Region, the counties most afflicted were Durham (6,235 acres) and Northumberland (3,969 acres). In Yorkshire, the West Riding (with 8,265 acres) had a most formidable problem. Derbyshire (4,997 acres) and Nottinghamshire (3,808 acres) had the highest incidence of dereliction in the North Midlands, but Northamptonshire, Leicestershire and Kesteven had appreciable problems. Essex (4,990 acres) had the greatest amount in the Eastern Region and there were large areas in Bedfordshire, Norfolk and Huntingdonshire. London and the Southern Region were least affected but there was a fair amount of dereliction in Dorset, Buckinghamshire and Oxfordshire. Cornwall (10,270 acres) had the heaviest incidence in the South Western Region, but both Somerset and Gloucestershire also had considerable areas affected. Of the dereliction in Cornwall, it was estimated that 78 per cent arose from the mining of metallic ores, 20 per cent from china clay workings and 2 per cent from granite quarrying. In the Midland Region, the largest amount was in Staffordshire (7,266 acres) but Shropshire and Warwickshire also had considerable problems. In the North Western Region, Lancashire (11,020 acres) supported the heaviest burden but Cheshire also had an appreciable amount. Most of the dereliction in the South Eastern Region was in Kent (4,583 acres). In Wales, the urban counties of Glamorganshire (4,438 acres) and Monmouthshire (4,118 acres) produced the highest returns but the rural counties of Cardiganshire, Denbighshire, Merioneth and Flintshire also contained extensive derelict areas.

Reviews of Development Plans

In order to stimulate the preparation of reclamation schemes the Ministry of Housing and Local Government (in Circular 9 of 1955) required all local planning authorities to make a detailed survey of all the derelict land within their administrative boundaries and to record the results in the first review documents of approved development plans. At the same time a programme of reclamation schemes was to be submitted. This request was reinforced in 1956 by Technical Memorandum No. 7 entitled 'Derelict Land and its Reclamation' which set out the various REF points for consideration in making a survey and the procedure for analysing the facts recorded in the survey. Accordingly it was assumed that eventually there would be a fully documented survey of all the dereliction in the country as well as a time-table for its reclamation; the latter perhaps being the more important.

However, in the development plan survey reports subsequently submitted, it was found that although the information about derelict land was useful for understanding the position in individual local authority areas, it was not possible to derive from it, at any one point in time, a full assessment of the total amount of dereliction in England and Wales or of the progress being made in dealing with it. This was largely due to the fact that surveys relate to different periods owing to the varying times of submission and also because little information was available of the action taken by each local authority to reclaim or otherwise treat the derelict land.

Therefore a further Circular (No. 55) was issued in September 1964 intimating that the Minister wished to compile comprehensive information about derelict land in a form which would enable it to be kept up to date, year by year. Accordingly, all local authorities were requested, in addition to the development plan review data, to complete and submit annually on 31st March a return of the derelict land in their areas in a form which categorized the dereliction and treatment under the headings of (1) Spoilheaps, (2) Excavations and pits, and (3) Other forms of dereliction. The local authority was required to assess the acreages of each of these forms of dereliction which (a) justified reclamation, (b) justified landscaping, and (c) did not require any treatment.

Introductory

Circular 55/64 also required completion of two other tables—one which set out the acreage of each category that had been (*a*) reclaimed and (*b*) landscaped during the preceding year—the second table required similar information regarding the acreage of each category intended to be dealt with in the succeeding year.

Explanatory notes attached to the circular excluded from the definition of derelict land and therefore from the return:

'(i) land such as tipping sites on which development has not been completed;

'(ii) land subject to conditions attached to planning permissions or other arrangements for restoration or landscaping;

'(iii) land which may be regarded as derelict from natural causes such as marshland and neglected woodland;

'(iv) war damaged land, "infilling" sites awaiting development and urban sites cleared with a view to redevelopment as part of a programme of urban renewal.'

The explanatory notes further directed that the assessment of dereliction should have particular regard to whether treatment of the site was desirable in the public interest, whether it was practicable (e.g. that sufficient filling material was likely to be available) and whether the work could be done at reasonable cost.

A county council could, by arrangement, complete the return on behalf of any county district council within the administrative county and many of the returns were so made by county councils.

The returns from local authorities in England, made in response to Circular No. 55/64 have now been processed and the final figures are summarized in Table II.

It will be appreciated that the new figures deriving from the Ministry's recent survey are significantly lower than those obtained by the survey in 1954. The intention of the recent survey was to identify the hard core of derelict land likely to be treated only if dealt with by public bodies, and local authorities were asked to exclude sites subject to planning conditions or

TABLE II.

Summary of Returns to Circular 55/64 from Local Authorities in England to the Ministry of Housing and Local Government

(i) Region	(ii) Spoil Heaps		(iii) Excavations and Pits		(iv) Other Forms of Dereliction		(v) Totals	
	Total Acreage	Acreage justifying treatment	Total Acreage	Acreage justifying treatment	Total Acreage	Acreage justifying treatment	Total Acreage	Acreage justifying treatment
North West	3,894	3,132	3,379	2,007	5,511	4,314	12,784	9,453
Northern	5,363	4,449	4,525	1,600	9,934	7,242	19,822	13,291
Yorkshire and Humberside	1,878	1,599	5,827	3,128	2,028	933	9,733	5,660
East Midlands	1,351	1,221	2,870	1,628	1,921	1,050	6,142	3,899
West Midlands	5,076	4,678	2,593	2,073	4,621	4,240	12,290	10,991
South West	13,122	1,796	1,417	322	1,503	645	16,042	2,763
South East	64	58	5,879	3,267	2,144	1,809	8,087	5,134
England	30,748	16,933	26,490	14,025	27,662	20,233	84,900	51,191
National Parks and Areas of Outstanding Natural Beauty	2,693	472	675	215	1,132	747	4,500	1,434
Development Districts	17,940	5,639	4,355	1,315	8,732	6,217	31,027	13,171

other statutory arrangements for restoration or landscaping. Also excluded in effect from the definition were sites on which development is still taking place and urban sites cleared as part of a programme of redevelopment. These exclusions are listed above. A further point of difference between the two surveys is that local authorities have now been asked to indicate how much of the land falling within the circular's definition it is desirable to treat in the public interest.

CHAPTER 2

Reclamation Incentives

Land Conservation

Land is one of the nation's basic assets and there is insufficient
to satisfy the demands upon it, consequently we can no longer
afford to waste it or to be prodigal in its use. It is the source of
our food supplies and the platform for all human activities. The
demands upon land are being increased by every form of user
and within the last decade or so, enormous demands have arisen
for quite new uses.

For the production of food, Britain has less than half an acre
per head of its population and this is a much smaller amount
than obtains in other countries. Two major wars and their aftermath during the first half of this century, clearly demonstrated
that the consequences of a land shortage involve a starvation
threat during wartime, and intensive industrial production and
export drives to pay for the importation of necessities during
peacetime. Agriculture, notwithstanding the much higher productivity it has attained, is continuously seeking more food-
producing land in order to support an ever-increasing population and in the effort to provide a greater proportion of home-
grown foodstuffs, so that the nation can become more self-
supporting.

More land is demanded for housing purposes and the multitude of ancillary uses that are essential to accommodate a
greater population. Furthermore the demands are swollen by
the higher standards of accommodation that now prevail, by the

earlier age of marriage and by the need to cope with a higher proportion of separate households. Over the next twenty years, it is estimated that at least six million more houses will be needed and however much building densities may be increased, the houses, garages, roads, car parks, shops, offices, schools, universities, hospitals, health centres, community halls, parks, playing fields, recreation grounds and all the other paraphernalia of urban living must cover more and more land, whether it be on the fringes of existing towns or the site of a new town.

The extractive industries—ironstone workings, sand and gravel pits, stone quarries, brick and tile marlholes, cement works and a host of others relying upon the winning of minerals have equipped themselves with larger and heavier machinery which works at a faster rate and eats further and quicker into the land. The early industrialists restored the land, as a matter of course, immediately after it had been worked. But as competition increased and the profit motive became predominant, the mineral wealth was extracted and the exhausted sites were abandoned; the entrepreneur moved on to a fresh site as soon as the old site fell behind in profitability, then the process was eventually repeated at the new site. The process is analogous to the bad husbandry which created 'dust bowls' by overcropping, exhausting soil nutrients, neglecting to apply fertilizers and then moving on to virgin land instead of practising conservation.

Manufacturing industry is making heavy demands on land; factories are being extended everywhere and new ones are being built continuously. Manufacturers and employees all want higher standards; more space, light and air as well as prestige buildings and front lawns. There is an insatiable demand for parking space, more playing fields, canteens and welfare facilities and there is a very marked preference for single-storey rather than multi-storey premises. Most of the old industrial areas have a tremendous backlog of obsolescent and slum factories which are overdue for redevelopment and when these are rebuilt they will conform to the more generous standards now prevalent.

Electricity generating stations, oil refineries, atomic energy establishments and their like, proliferate and make fresh demands and each new demand is a monster bite into the land. A modern power station of 2,000 M.W. capacity covers some five hundred acres with its buildings, sidings and cooling towers. An oil refinery takes a thousand acres or more and an atomic energy establishment affects an even greater area. It is becoming increasingly more difficult to accommodate these large land demands and those for airfields, airports and dock extensions. Of late years the extensive relinquishments of land formerly held by the Defence Services has helped substantially to meet fresh requirements but the Service holdings are now running down against an ascending demand.

We have no vast virgin open spaces to draw upon—on the contrary—we have a strictly limited area, a sea-girt island, a tight little island. Britain has been and is forced to plan its use of land in the most economical manner and every remedy must be applied which can ease land shortage and the pressures upon its use. Some land must be made to serve a number of purposes simultaneously where this is feasible and where the purposes do not conflict. The uplands and more marginal land must be brought under some form of cultivation and gradually into agricultural production. Afforestation will take on after agriculture and the timber line should creep higher up our hills and mountains as it has done already in other countries, some of which are not subject to such high land pressures as obtain in this country. Every kind of development may take place at higher densities—in any case the densities will be as high as is compatible with those standards which have been proven by experience, for these standards represent what is tolerable and what can be profitably provided. The extractive industries will work to a phased programme to avoid sterilization of land by excessive reservations. Land use design, zonings and careful layouts will obviate overlapping and wasteful forms of development and reduce reservations for hypothetical requirements. No waste of land can be countenanced and an appreciable contribution to the general economy can be made by bringing back all existing derelict industrial land into beneficial use.

The Pursuit of Prosperity

The blighting effect of derelict land extends far beyond the boundaries of the wasted area and oppresses the whole of the surrounding district. Where there is a concentration of dereliction the whole of a region can be detrimentally affected. Any tourist appeal the district may have had is rapidly lost. Then the depressing effects upon the inhabitants become manifest, people move away from the area and an atmosphere of decay sets in. The district becomes unattractive to industrialists and no new industrial development takes the place of the declining basic industries. Districts which are afflicted with a large share of dereliction become more and more handicapped in the endless competition for increased productivity and prosperity and eventually they fall behind even in the struggle for survival. Such districts become poorer and poorer and quite unable to meet the cost of reclamation schemes. What could have been accomplished in their prosperity becomes quite impossible in their decline. This retrogression has been repeatedly demonstrated in worked-out industrial areas. Attention has been focused recently on this trend in the North-East where reclamation of derelict land has been recognized as a vital element in rehabilitation and revival of the area. Industrial areas which are not retrograde are well aware of these tendencies and so the urge to maintain the prosperity of a district becomes another incentive to undertake reclamation.

The Incentive of Past Achievements

Notwithstanding little encouragement or co-ordination in the distant past, an astonishing amount of reclamation has already been achieved under most adverse conditions. (See Plate 7.) Of the earliest reclamation work—that carried out by the industrialists themselves—few records remain, but there are some examples to be seen in the Midlands. One of the first recorded was the afforestation in 1815 of abandoned limestone workings at

Dudley Castle Hill, Wren's Nest and Mons Hill by the Earl of Dudley. These three hills have been conspicuous landmarks for generations and since their afforestation they have served as highly appreciated amenity features for the surrounding districts. Other similar examples occurred at Hawne Colliery, Halesowen; Haden Hill and Timbertree Mound, Cradley Heath and Moxley Hospital grounds, Bilston. The Midland Reafforesting Association was formed in 1903 and did most creditable work until it was dissolved in 1924. Thus in the Midlands it is possible to point to examples which demonstrate that the areas of spoliation of one generation can become beauty spots to succeeding generations.

Since the end of the 1939–1945 war, a new epoch may be said to have commenced—one in which the employment of heavy earth-moving equipment became an outstanding feature. Pioneer work was again done in the Black Country, in the Potteries and in Coalbrookdale. A little later in the early fifties, the West Riding, Durham and Lancashire followed with laudable reclamation programmes and throughout the whole period, restoration after opencast coal working and ironstone working has provided notable examples of successful work. Now an extensive reclamation programme is getting under way in the North-East.

The Black Country

Smoke, engineering skill and derelict land seem always to have been concomitant features of the Black Country. In 1946 Professor S. H. Beaver was commissioned by the Minister of Town and Country Planning to make a survey of the derelict land in the Black Country. His report outlined the problems and scheduled 9,277 acres (more than one acre in every eight) as derelict in a broad sense. Of this total, 6,102 acres were classified as chronic dereliction and the hardcore of the problem. There was at the same time in the Black Country, the post-war housing problem and a paramount need to solve it. Local Authorities and Government Departments co-operated in solution of these twin problems by reclamation of derelict sites for housing purposes (see Plate 8) instead of using virgin land for the extensive municipal estates which arose. The work was pursued with

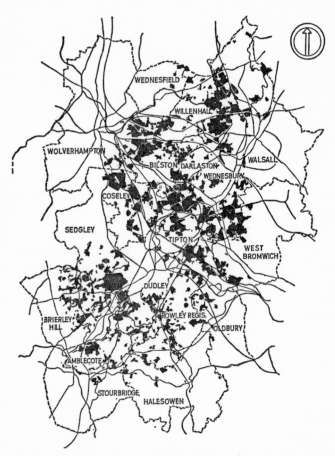

Fig 4 Derelict land. The Black Country

vigour and within five years over three thousand acres of derelict land were reclaimed in the Black Country alone. (See Plates 9 and 10.) The good work has gone on and today over six thousand acres have been reclaimed. The following table shows the position in each local authority's area at the beginning of 1964. (All figures represent acreages.)

TABLE III. **Reclamation in the Black Country**

Local Authority	Administrative Area	Amount of Derelict Land	Amount Reclaimed	Residue
County Boroughs				
Dudley	4,328	822	605	217
Smethwick	2,500	17	17	Nil
Walsall	8,777	1,002	730	272
West Bromwich	7,172	992	785	207
Wolverhampton	9,126	436	355	81
Municipal Boroughs				
Bilston	1,869	552	450	102
Halesowen	5,247	109	26	83
Oldbury	3,300	173	71	102
Rowley Regis	3,793	723	299	424
Stourbridge	4,214	74	54	20
Tipton	2,167	479	309	170
Wednesbury	2,025	522	446	76
Urban Districts				
Amblecote	665	64	5	59
Brierley Hill	5,851	1,048	421	627
Coseley	3,168	1,061	725	336
Darlaston	1,535	520	364	156
Sedgley	3,830	307	102	205
Wednesfield	2,515	215	57	158
Willenhall	2,834	612	324	288
Totals	74,916	9,728	6,145	3,583

The Potteries

No less than the Black Country, the Potteries have possessed the concomitant characteristics of smoke, manufacturing skill and derelict land. (See Plates 11 and 12.) Little was done to remedy the adverse features of this region until after the war but since that time there has been an awakening of the civic consciousness which has resulted in a tremendous improvement in environmental conditions throughout the Potteries. Replacement of the old smoky bottle kilns by electrically and gas fired tunnel kilns has vastly reduced atmospheric pollution and cleared the skies. During 1948 a reclamation programme com-

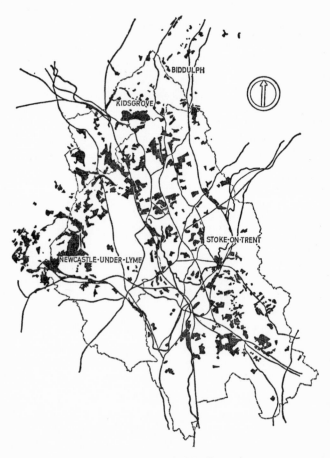

Fig 5 Derelict land. The Potteries

menced in Stoke on Trent and an increasing amount of work has been done throughout North Staffordshire as can be seen from the following table which gives the situation at the beginning of 1964. (All figures represent acreages.)

TABLE IV. **Reclamation in the Potteries**

Local Authority	Administrative Area	Amount of Derelict Land	Amount Reclaimed	Residue
Stoke on Trent County Borough	21,190	2,302	983	1,319
Newcastle under Lyme Municipal Borough	8,882	1,096	268	828
Biddulph Urban District	6,647	74	26	48
Kidsgrove Urban District	4,095	551	220	331
Cheadle Rural District	60,291	74	13	61
Newcastle under Lyme Rural District	40,121	384	143	241
Totals	141,226	4,481	1,653	2,828

Coalbrookdale

This district around Ironbridge has a niche in English social history as the birthplace of the industrial revolution and it deserves a better memorial to the enterprise of its past than despoiled acres slowly yielding to the mellowing influences of time. Since the decline in the region's fortunes, the local authorities concerned have been unable financially to undertake reclamation schemes and so most of the abandoned mounds remain more than a century later, still acquiring a scanty covering of rough grass and scrub. A covering which has little aesthetic and less economic value but which at least serves to remove rawness and softens the harsh scarring of this Shropshire countryside. A survey of this part of East Shropshire was carried out during 1946 by Mr. N. Bennett the County Planning Officer and 2,782 acres were then scheduled as derelict. The reclamation carried out up to the beginning of 1964 is shown in the following table. (All figures represent acreages.)

At long last, this district will have a fitting acknowledgement of the part it played in the early industrial history of the nation, when a new town is built at Dawley (*vide* p. 188). New life will stir in the dead acres and prosperity will return to a neglected

region when Dawley emerges phoenix-like to demonstrate how
a devastated area and a decayed environment can be renewed

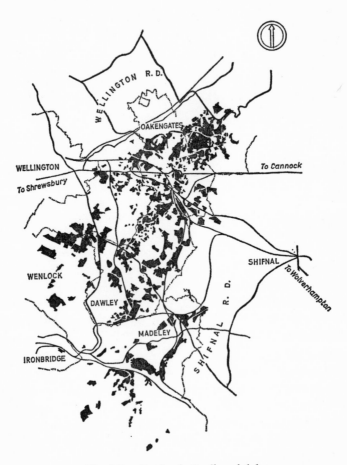

Fig 6 Derelict land. Coalbrookdale

with singular distinction, and at the same time make another
contribution to the national welfare by accommodating overspill from an overcrowded city thirty miles away.

TABLE V. **Reclamation in Coalbrookdale**

Local Authority	Administrative Area	Amount of Derelict Land	Amount Reclaimed	Residue
Wenlock Municipal Borough	22,657	483	78	405
Dawley Urban District	3,259	836	320	516
Oakengates Urban District	2,396	673	182	491
Shifnal Rural District	39,562	57	Nil	57
Wellington Rural District	54,584	733	164	569
Totals	122,458	2,782	744	2,038

Recreational Demands

With the shorter working week and the increase of population there is bound to be an enormous increase in the demands for more recreational space and far more will be required in every district than the playing fields envisaged in the standards promulgated by the National Playing Fields Association. No better social use could be found for derelict land than its employment to meet this recreational demand and in linking these two problems of dereliction and the provision of amenity it is again demonstrated that derelict land should be regarded as a challenge and an opportunity rather than as dead land and a liability which of course it is until redeemed.

Much of the land so far restored has been utilized for residential or industrial development, largely because special grants for reclamation have not been available, and the most profitable form of development has often had to be found in order to render a scheme economically possible and likely to be carried out at all. An analysis of early work in the Black Country was made in a paper presented by the author to the Public Works Congress in 1952 and this showed that 64 per cent of the reclamation had been undertaken for housing purposes, 20 per cent had been carried out for industrial purposes, 13 per cent had been used for public open-space purposes, and 3 per cent accommodated schools and public buildings. An analysis made at

47

the same time of post-reclamation uses in the Potteries revealed quite different proportions and a wider range of uses because only 40 per cent had been redeveloped for housing purposes, 18 per cent had been devoted to public open space, 17 per cent had been utilized for industrial development, 15 per cent had been used for schools and school playing fields and 10 per cent had reverted to agriculture. A recent analysis in the Potteries has shown that use for residential purposes had fallen still further to 28 per cent while industrial redevelopment has increased to 25 per cent. There must be wide variations in the post-reclamation uses depending upon the demand prevailing in the locality at the time and frequently it depends upon the profitability or otherwise of a scheme. But so far there is no doubt the emphasis has been upon housing and industrial uses, notwithstanding the fact that a great many of the districts afflicted with derelict land are at the same time notably deficient in open space for recreational purposes even by the standards of the National Playing Fields Association.

Land in its derelict state frequently serves as a kind of open space and even as a recreational area, particularly where it is not fenced or enclosed. Hosts of children may be accustomed to play on it, people go for walks upon it or they may regularly take the dog for a walk along the 'banks'. When it forms part of some urban blight it is almost invariably located in the midst of congested housing and slum factories where there is the greatest deficiency of public open and playing fields. If such a site is reclaimed and built over, there may be what amounts to a reduction of available open space where it can least be afforded, because however much an eyesore the site might have been, it was still an asset in a densely built-up area in so far as it functioned as an open space 'lung'.

The blighting effect of derelict land upon the whole of its surrounding district makes the desirability of its restoration obvious and the general shortage of land makes its utilization for some good purpose essential. This purpose is perhaps generally its most profitable use, but there should be an exception in all densely built-up areas where there is a deficiency in public open

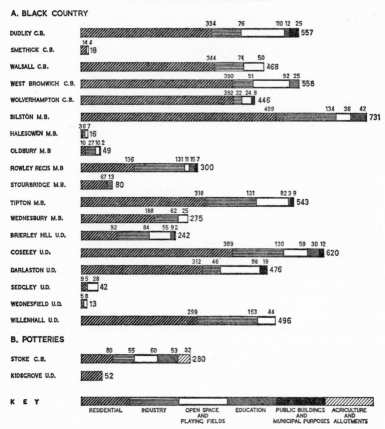

Fig 7. Subsequent uses of restored land.
Figures represent acreages

space. In any case it could well be the accepted policy that when a local authority commits itself to expenditure on a reclamation scheme, at least a proportion of the restored land should be devoted to an open space use, preferably of a recreational nature. Such a policy would be even more appropriate in those cases where reclamation has been undertaken by public sub-scription. Where level sites become available they should cer-tainly be reserved for playing fields but where the sites are rugged and broken they can still serve without being subjected to heavy levelling or expensive treatment. They are far better left as timbered hillocks or depressions to serve, according to their size, as adventure play areas for children for the smaller sites and as picnic places or landscape features of public resort for the larger sites. There is an ever increasing need for these places and yet under present conditions, local authorities are more and more reluctant to acquire land at the prevalent high valuations for existing uses and the current market prices in order to devote it to non-remunerative uses such as public open space or recreation areas.

Notwithstanding the high costs of acquisition and the expense of reclamation—any money spent in this way by a local authority would be as well spent as that used in providing National Parks and Conservation Areas. For the conversion of derelict land to open space for recreational purposes in and near densely populated areas creates a local amenity feature which is likely to be enjoyed continuously by relatively greater numbers than can enjoy the National Parks and Conservation Areas which are of necessity more remote and therefore capable of giving enjoyment to fewer people on occasional holidays.

CHAPTER 3

Legal and Financial Provisions

Local authorities are not under any statutory obligation to reclaim the derelict land which may exist within their administrative boundaries, but they have various powers scattered over a number of Acts which enable them to do so and they have, of course, a general responsibility for the welfare of their districts while local planning authorities are responsible for the good planning of their areas and making provision for the best use of land.

The Town and Country Planning Act 1944, Section 10(3) empowered local authorities to acquire derelict land 'with a view to securing that it is brought into use', but this specific power was repealed by the Town and Country Planning Act 1947 and it has not been re-enacted in subsequent legislation. Until the Local Authorities (Land) Act 1963 became operative, local authorities had to rely entirely upon powers they possessed under a wide variety of enactments to acquire derelict land. They could acquire it for the purposes of housing, education, refuse disposal, the provision of public open space or another of their statutory functions. Having acquired the land they could reclaim it for the purpose for which it had been acquired. They could not acquire the land solely because it happened to be derelict nor could they acquire it for a purpose outside their statutory functions, such as the provision of a factory site.

The main provisions, relevant to derelict land, at present operative, are to be found in the National Parks and Access to the Countryside Act 1949; the Mineral Workings Act 1951; the

51

Local Employment Act 1960; the Town and Country Planning Act 1962 and the Local Authorities (Land) Act 1963. These provisions are briefly described below.

The National Parks and Access to the Countryside Act 1949

This Act made provision for National Parks and the establishment of a National Parks Commission. It conferred upon the Nature Conservancy and local authorities, powers for the establishment and maintenance of nature reserves. It made provision for the recording, creation, maintenance and improvement of public paths and amended the law relating to rights of way. It conferred powers for preserving and enhancing the natural beauty of England and Wales. With respect to nature conservation it applies to Scotland.

Section 89(2) empowered a local planning authority to (*a*) plant trees or (*b*) carry out such work or do such other things as appear to them expedient for the purpose of restoring or improving the appearance of derelict land in their area which in their opinion is in any way unsightly.

Section 89(3) enabled the powers to be exercised by an authority, either on land belonging to them or on other land with the consent of all persons interested therein.

Section 89(4) contains a saving for the powers of the council of any county, county borough or county district under any other enactment.

Section 89(5) enables a local planning authority to acquire land compulsorily for the purpose of any of their functions under Section 89.

Section 89(6) provides that where a local planning authority exercise their powers under Section 89, on land not belonging to the authority, the management of the land, so far as it relates to anything done by the authority, may be undertaken by the authority or by a person interested in the land, on such terms as may be agreed between the authority and the interested persons.

Section 102(1) gives power to authorize other local authorities to act in place of a local planning authority, where this is expedient. In default of agreement between the local authority and local planning authority, the Minister may determine. The Section therefore extends to local authorities the powers to acquire land and to undertake ameliorating works, provided they obtain the consent of the local planning authority, or a direction of the Minister.

(*b*) Exchequer Grants

Section 97 of this Act in conjunction with the Grant Regulations authorizes the Minister of Housing and Local Government to pay grants of up to 75 per cent of the expenditure incurred by local authorities in exercise of the powers conferred under Section 89, but only where this expenditure relates to land within national parks or areas of outstanding natural beauty. According to the Grant Regulations explanatory memorandum 'the precise nature of the works which will be approved for grant purposes will be determined according to the circumstances in each individual case'.

The Mineral Workings Act 1951

Under the provisions of this Act, a fund was established for financing the restoration of land made derelict by opencast ironstone workings before the advent of full planning control under the Town and Country Planning Act 1947. The Act also provides arrangements for dealing with expenditure on the restoration of land subject to current workings for ironstone extraction, including its cultivation and afforestation.

Section 1 defines the 'ironstone district' as the counties of Leicester, Lincoln (Kesteven and Lindsey), Northampton, Oxford, Rutland, Warwick and the Soke of Peterborough, but the Minister is empowered to add other areas.

The Ironstone Restoration Fund under control of the Minister of Housing and Local Government is authorized by Section 2. This fund is financed by basic contributions from operators of 1⅛d. per ton of ironstone extracted (Section 3). Annual returns of ironstone production must be made to the Minister and payments made to the fund accordingly (Section 4). Ironstone owners and landowners deriving royalties are required to contribute a similar amount to the Fund, in accordance with the formula of the Second Schedule (Section 5). Land held by charitable trusts is exempted by Section 7. Under Section 8, the Exchequer makes a contribution to the Fund of $\frac{3}{4}$d. per ton. In effect, about 75 per cent of the Fund is provided by the ironstone operators and royalty owners jointly, and the national funds contribute approximately 25 per cent.

Ironstone operators carrying out restoration works are entitled, under Section 9, to payments from the Fund in respect of such works. The payments are made at a rate per acre which represents the amount by which the cost per acre incurred by the operator (working efficiently with normal plant) exceeds the standard rate of £110 per acre. That is, the ore producer is under a statutory obligation to bear the first £110 per acre of restoration costs, and payments from the Fund meet the additional costs.

Any local authority within the 'ironstone district' is empowered by Section 16 to carry out levelling, tree planting or other works for restoring or improving the appearance or screening from view, the worked ironstone land or affected neighbouring land. Section 16(2) enables these works to be carried out by a local authority, either on land owned by them or other land with the consent of all persons interested and upon terms agreed between them. Section 17 empowers a local authority to acquire land by agreement or compulsorily. Section 18 empowers the Minister to make grants to local authorities in respect of restoration works. Provision is also made for meeting the costs of any subsequent agricultural or forestry operations which may be necessary.

Section 20 empowers the Minister of Agriculture and Fisheries to make arrangements for the management and farming of land in order to bring it into a good state of cultivation and fertility and Section 23 confers powers of compulsory acquisition for the purposes of agriculture.

Legal and Financial Provisions

Section 27 gives the Minister default powers and Section 28 authorizes modifications of payments in lieu of restoration under ironstone leases. Section 32 provides for the temporary stopping up of highways and Section 36 gives powers of entry to land.

The Local Employment Act 1960

This enactment is primarily designed to promote employment in localities where high and persistent unemployment exists or is threatened.

By Section 1, the powers available under this Act are restricted to land within a 'development district' which is defined as any locality in Great Britain where, in the opinion of the Board of Trade, a high rate of unemployment exists, or is to be expected within such period as it is expedient to exercise powers under the Act, and (in either case) is likely to persist, whether seasonally or generally. The development districts at present designated include the Ministry of Labour employment exchange areas in the North-East (Tyne and Tees), West Cumberland, Yorkshire, North-West (Merseyside), South-West (Cornwall and North Devon), North Wales (Anglesey, Carnarvon), South Wales and Monmouthshire, Clydeside, Highlands and Islands, Lanarkshire, etc. The list varies from time to time according to the unemployment situation and the Board of Trade must be consulted to ascertain the current position at any one time.

In exercising their powers under the Act, the Board of Trade must have regard to (a) the relationship between the expenditure involved and the employment likely to be provided and (b) any consequential effect on employment in other development districts.

Section 5 deals with derelict land and contains provisions respecting land in a development district, where it appears to the Board of Trade that by reason of its being derelict, neglected or unsightly, and likely to remain so for a considerable period, it is expedient that steps should be taken to bring the land into use or to improve the amenities of the neighbourhood. Section 5(2) empowers the Board to acquire such land by agreement or compulsorily and the Board may carry out any work on the land as appears to them expedient, for enabling it to be brought into use or for improving the amenities of the neighbourhood. The Act does not confer these powers upon local authorities who must proceed by powers available under other legislation.

Under Section 5(3) the Minister of Housing and Local Government (with consent of the Treasury) is empowered to make grants to local authorities in development districts for the reclamation of derelict, neglected or unsightly land. Such grants may be made towards the costs of acquisition of the land as well as towards the costs of remedial works which are necessary to enable the land to be brought into use or to improve the local amenities. It is a condition of any grant, that the works should be expedient for the purpose of improving the district and making it more attractive to industry, thereby increasing the employment potential of that district. If the local authority does not already own the site, it should be acquired before any works commence. The amount of grant is not prescribed by the Act and it can vary from time to time, according to what is requisite in the opinion of the Minister of Housing and Local Government, to implement the requirements of Section 5(3). At present (December 1964) the grant is at the rate of 85 per cent of the approved net cost, in addition to any rate deficiency grant attracted by the expenditure, but subject to the aggregate Exchequer assistance not exceeding 95 per cent under both grants. The Act provides that the statutory powers under which this grant is payable expire on 31st March 1967 unless Parliament otherwise determines. Circular 30/50 issued by the Ministry of Housing and Local Government in April 1960 contains useful information and advice.

The Town and Country Planning Act 1962

This is a codifying Act which consolidates the previous enactments relating to town and country planning in England and Wales and accordingly repeals the Town and Country Planning

Plate 6. Opencast coal site at Ewart Hill

Plate 7. An early reclamation scheme. Manual labour with picks and shovels, horses and jubilee trucks, levelling a slag heap at Park Lane Estate, Wednesbury, 1932

Plate 8. Reclamation for housing development of Old Park, Dudley, Worcestershire

Plate 9. Hampstead Colliery Pit, West Bromwich, 1948. Note erosion gulleys and reference points of chimneys behind spoilheap and goal post in front

Plate 10. Hampstead Colliery Tip being levelled, 1952

Plate 11. A typical area in the Potteries, including parts of Cobridge, Hanley and Etruria. Vertical air photograph showing tips, marlholes, subsidence flashes, steelworks, colliery and potteries

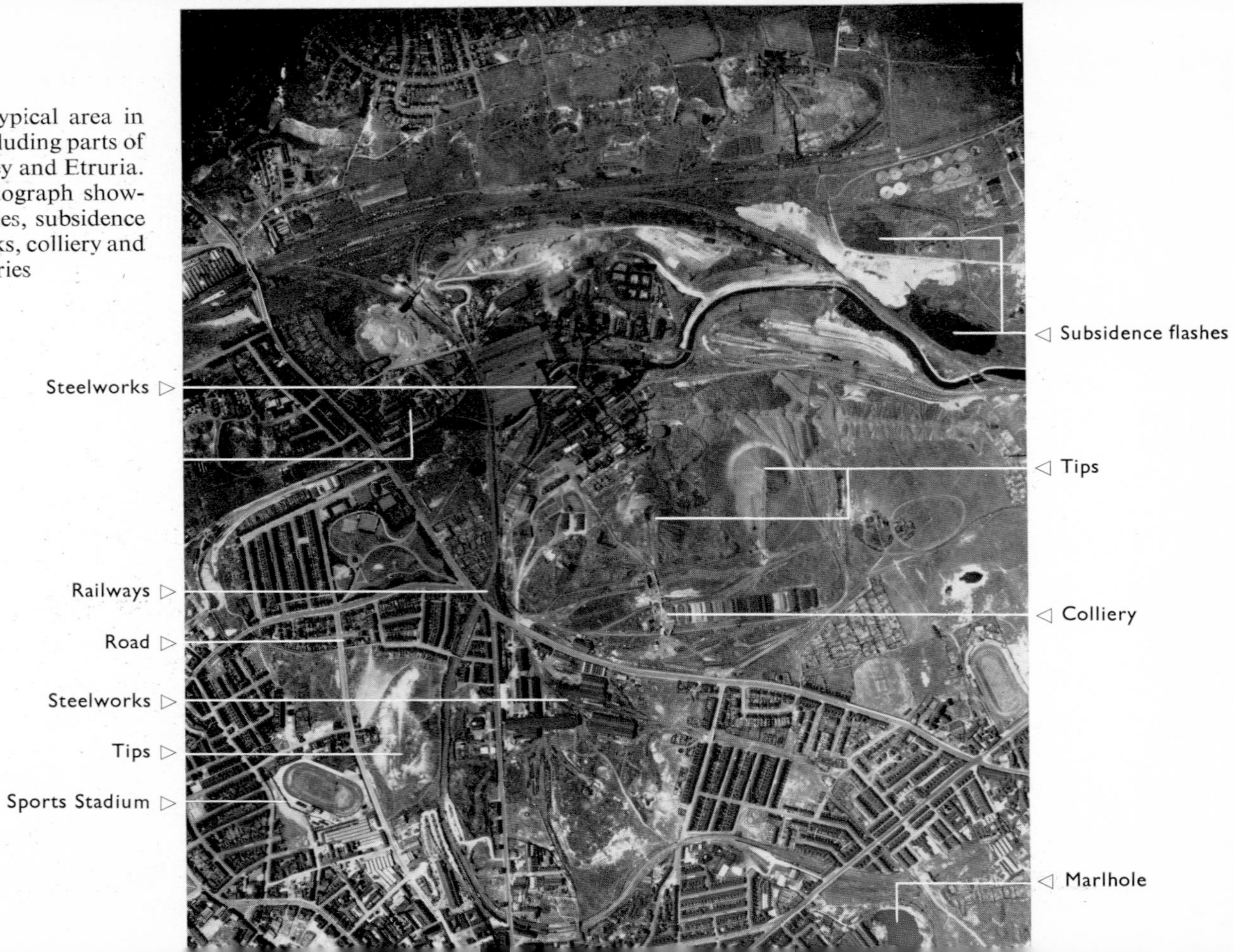

△ Subsidence flashes

△ Tips

△ Colliery

△ Marlhole

Steelworks △

Railways △

Road △

Steelworks △

Tips △

Sports Stadium △

▽ Colliery

▽ Railway

▽ Steelworks

▽ Tips

Steelworks ▽

Potteries ▽

Road ▽

Sports
Stadium ▽

Plate 12. Oblique air photograph of the same area in the Potteries. Road, railway, steelworks and colliery marked as reference points in both photographs

Plate 13. A Colliery near Barnsley

Plate 14. Worked out gravel pit at Besthorpe on the Trent being filled by pulverized fuel ash from High Marnham power station

Plate 15. Adjoining gravel pit at Besthorpe already filled by pulverized fuel ash from the High Marnham generating station

Plate 16. Peterborough brickworks showing flooded marlholes at Fletton, 1948

Plate 17. Peterborough brickworks. Land reclamation scheme in progress during 1963, using pulverized fuel ash for filling

Acts of 1944, 1951, 1953, and most of the provisions of the Town and Country Planning Acts of 1947, 1954, and 1959.

Derelict land is not specifically dealt with but Section 68 confers upon local authorities, powers for the compulsory acquisition of land for development, provided the Minister is satisfied that it is necessary that the land should be acquired for 'securing its use in the manner proposed by the plan'. Section 71 enables local authorities to purchase land by agreement in order to secure its use in accordance with the provisions of the development plan. If the development plan does not show the use intended for the land on redevelopment, it will be necessary in order to acquire the land to submit a formal amendment to the plan showing that use.

These powers of acquisition are regarded as also enabling the land to be cleared, levelled, graded and generally rendered suitable for redevelopment. The subsequent works of redevelopment usually depend upon other more specific powers such as the Housing Act 1957 for housing projects, the Education Act 1944 for schools and either the Public Health Act 1875 or the Open Spaces Act 1906 for public open space. Where land has been acquired and put into a condition enabling it to be redeveloped, it sometimes happens that the local authority desires a certain type of development for which it has no powers, such as industrial, commercial or agricultural uses. In such cases, if the land has been acquired for planning purposes (see table, page 62) such development may be undertaken, with consent of the Minister, under Section 79 of the Town and Country Planning Act 1962. Alternatively Section 2 of the Local Authorities (Land) Act 1963 might be helpful in such circumstances inasmuch as it permits a local authority, with consent of the Minister, to erect any building and carry out works on land for the benefit and improvement of the district.

Neglected Sites

Although rarely likely to be applicable to derelict land, it should be noted in passing that Section 36 of the Town and

Introductory

Country Planning Act 1962 empowers a local planning authority to require proper maintenance of waste land in the following terms—

'If it appears to a local planning authority that the amenity of any part of their area, or of any adjoining area, is seriously injured by the condition of any garden, vacant site or other open land in their area, then, subject to any directions given by the Minister, the authority may serve on the owner and occupier of the land a notice requiring such steps for abating the injury as may be specified in the notice to be taken within such period as may be so specified.'

The Local Authorities (Land) Act 1963

This Act contains a number of miscellaneous provisions amending the law relating to the functions of local authorities affecting land, extending generally, powers which were previously only available in local Acts.

Section 1 extends the power of local authorities to acquire land by agreement for local Act purposes as well as for functions under public general Acts. Except in the case of acquisitions outside an authority's own area, the Minister's consent is no longer needed to acquisitions in advance of requirements.

Section 2 empowers local authorities for the benefit or improvement of their districts to erect any building and construct or carry out works on land held by them. These powers are complementary to the power in Section 79 of the Town and Country Planning Act 1962 which empowers local authorities to carry out development on land held for planning purposes. Consent of the Minister is necessary to the use of powers under this Section and the Minister may require any application to be advertised. Section 2(4) empowers a local authority to repair, maintain and insure any building or works erected and generally to deal with them in a proper course of management. The powers contained in this section should not be used where the work can more appropriately be carried out under other specific statutory powers.

Section 6 extends the provisions of Section 89 of the National

Parks and Access to the Countryside Act 1949, so that 'where it appears to a local authority that any land in their area is derelict, neglected or unsightly, they may carry out such work as appears to them expedient for the purpose of enabling the land to be brought into use or improving the appearance of the land'. In national parks and areas of outstanding natural beauty, however, these powers are available only to the local planning authority for the area in which the land is situate, unless under Section 102 of the 1949 Act the powers are exercisable by another local authority.

Section 6(2) enables the powers contained in Section 6(1) to be exercised notwithstanding the availability of appropriate powers in other statutes.

Section 6(3) restricts the powers of compulsory purchase contained in Section 89(5) of the National Parks Act 1949 (which are now available to all local authorities) to cases where the Minister 'is satisfied that the land is derelict or that by reason of neglect following the abandonment of the previous use', the land is and is likely to continue in such a condition, that acquisition is desirable in the public interest.

Miscellaneous Enactments

The foregoing provisions are the main powers and sanctions available in connection with reclamation schemes but scattered throughout the Statute Book are other miscellaneous enactments which are occasionally relevant and can sometimes be brought into service. *The Local Government Act 1933* Section 157 gives local authorities a general power to acquire land by agreement and Section 159 empowers local authorities to purchase land compulsorily for the purposes of any of their statutory functions.

Where a site will eventually be developed for housing purposes it may be acquired by agreement under Sections 96 and 97 of the *Housing Act 1957*. If compulsory acquisition is necessary, the powers are available in Section 97. Authority for carrying out works of clearance and site preparation is derived from

Introductory

Sections 92 and 93. County Councils and Parish Councils are not housing authorities and therefore they cannot, of course, operate any of these powers.

For schools and school playing fields, all Education Authorities have powers of compulsory acquisition in Section 90 of the *Education Act 1944* and they are empowered to carry out works by the provisions contained in Sections 9, 13 and 40 to 43.

Land can be acquired by agreement for use as public open space in the form of parks, recreation grounds or playing fields under the provisions of Sections 9 and 14 of the *Open Spaces Act 1906* or under Section 4 of the *Physical Training and Recreation Act 1937*. Compulsory acquisition powers are contained in Section 5 of the Physical Training and Recreation Act 1937. All local authorities may utilize these powers, but a Parish Council must first obtain consent of its County Council. Authorization for the execution of works upon the land is available in Sections 10 and 14 of the Open Spaces Act 1906 or Section 4 of the Physical Training and Recreation Act 1937 or Section 164 of the *Public Health Act 1875*.

All local authorities, except County Councils and Parish Councils, can acquire land compulsorily and carry out works upon the land so that it may be developed as a site for the parking of cars, under the powers contained in Section 81 of the *Road Traffic Act 1960*.

Where a site is required for refuse disposal purposes, it may be acquired compulsorily by any local authority except a County Council or Parish Council under the provisions of Section 306 of the *Public Health Act 1936*. Any works of site preparation which may be required are authorized under the provisions of Section 76 of the Public Health Act 1936.

Sites upon which it is intended to erect public buildings or offices may be acquired compulsorily and developed by all local authorities except Parish Councils, under the provisions of Section 125 of the *Local Government Act 1933*.

Many local authorities have promoted *Local Acts* which have conferred upon them powers to acquire land by agreement 'for the benefit, improvement and development of the district'. This wide power can cover almost every voluntary acquisition of derelict land, for those local authorities who enjoy it. These powers of acquisition normally carry collateral powers for clearing the site and making it fit for the redevelopment purpose. However, the redevelopment works themselves must normally be carried out under the general Act powers regulating some statutory function of the local authority, such as housing, provision of schools or public open space.

FINANCIAL ASSISTANCE

No specific Exchequer assistance in respect of derelict land reclamation costs is generally available.

The general grant system introduced under the Local Government Act 1958 replaced specific grants which had formerly been available to local authorities on expenditure incurred for particular purposes (e.g. Section 93 of the Town and Country Planning Act 1947—a purpose that could have included derelict land reclamation under the powers of that Act). This general grant is now in the form of a block grant to County and County Borough Councils, based upon a formula that is set out in the General Grants Order. The recipient authorities can themselves determine the re-allocation of the block grant to meet the cost of each of the services they provide, and in the case of county councils, the re-allocation includes the contributions towards the costs of services provided by each of the constituent county district councils.

A rate deficiency grant is payable under Section 7 of the Local Government Act 1958, to all those local authorities whose rate resources are below average. The amount of grant is assessed as a percentage of expenditure and it depends upon the total expenditure of the local authority how great is the deficiency of the rate product as compared with the national average. Where a local authority qualifying for this grant carries out derelict land reclamation, the authority receives in the grant a percentage of its expenditure on reclamation work.

TABLE VI. Principal powers of Local Authorities to acquire land and carry out works on it

Purposes	Acquisition by agreement	Compulsory Acquisition	Works Authorization	Type of authority
Planning	Town and Country Planning Act 1962 Section 71. The land must be shown in approved development plan for the use proposed.	Town and Country Planning Act 1962 Section 68(1). Land must be shown in approved development plan for the use proposed and designated for compulsory purchase	Section 79	All local authorities (except parish councils) where acquisition is by agreement. Authority in whose area the land is situate or by other authority authorized by the Minister to acquire
National Parks	Local Government Act 1933 Section 157	National Parks and Access to the Countryside Act 1949. Section 89(5)	Section 89(1)	Local Planning Authorities
Local Act functions Improvement of district	Local Authorities (Land) Act 1963 Section 1	Local Authorities (Land) Act 1963 Section 6(3) in conjunction with section 89(5) of the National Parks and Access to the Countryside Act 1949	Section 2	Local authorities
General Statutory functions	Local Government Act 1933 Section 157	Local Government Act 1933 Section 159		Local authorities
Housing and ancillary	Housing Act 1957 Section 96	Housing Act 1957 section 97	Sections 92, 93, and 126	Housing authorities

Purposes	Acquisition by agreement	Compulsory Acquisition	Works Authorization	Type of authority
Education	Education Act 1944 Section 90	Education Act 1944 Section 90	Sections 9, 13, 40-43 and 53	Education authorities
Open Space	Open Spaces Act 1906 Sections 9 and 14		Sections 10 and 14	All authorities
Recreation	Physical Training and Recreation Act 1937 Section 4	Physical Training and Recreation Act 1937 Section 5	Physical Training and Recreation Act 1937 Section 4 and Public Health Act 1875 Section 164	All authorities
Refuse disposal	Local Government Act 1933 Section 157	Public Health Act 1936 Section 306	Public Health Act 1936 Section 76	All authorities except county councils and parish councils
Car Parks	Local Government Act 1933 Section 157	Road Traffic Act 1960 Section 81	Road Traffic Act 1960 Section 81	All authorities except county councils and parish councils
Municipal Buildings	Local Government Act 1933 Section 157	Local Government Act 1933 Section 125	Section 125	All authorities except parish councils
Smallholdings	Agricultural Act 1947 Section 48	Agricultural Act 1947 Section 48	Section 48	County Councils only

Introductory

As there are diverse provisions in many Acts which cover the acquisition and development of land for the statutory functions of local authorities, so there are various provisions under which some form or other of financial assistance may be available to meet the costs of reclamation schemes. The powers of the National Parks and Access to the Countryside Act 1949 are exercisable in any part of the country and they enable local authorities to undertake minor works for ameliorating dereliction by a general tidying up and by tree planting or landscaping, but grant is only payable in respect of land within the confines of a national park or area of outstanding natural beauty. Similarly financial assistance from the Ironstone Restoration Fund under the Mineral Workings Act 1951 is only available within the ironstone district. Grants under the Local Employment Act 1960 are only available within development districts as extended by Section 1(4) of that Act.

Under the Local Government Act 1948, Section 126, a County Council (with consent of the Minister of Housing and Local Government) may make a contribution towards the expenses incurred by one of its County District Councils in reclaiming derelict land, where this would be reasonable having regard to the financial resources of the County District Council. A few County Councils have made generous arrangements with their County District Councils.

Where derelict land may be reclaimed by a local authority in pursuance of a town development scheme to accommodate overspill population and relieve congestion, the Minister of Housing and Local Government may contribute to the expenses of the receiving local authority in accordance with the provisions of Section 2 of the Town Development Act 1952.

Under the Housing Act 1961, an 'expensive site subsidy' is payable in respect of all dwellings approved for subsidy under the Act, whether they are erected by local authorities, housing associations or other agencies, when the cost of purchasing and developing a site exceeds £4,000 an acre. Part of the cost might be due to the use of derelict land which has had to be reclaimed before the site could be used for the purpose of providing houses or flats. The amount of the subsidy varies according to the total site costs. For sites costing more than £4,000 but less than £5,000 an acre, the subsidy is £60 per acre per annum for sixty years. From that point, the subsidy is progressively increased by £34 per acre for each £1,000 (or part) by which the cost per acre exceeds £5,000. Thus for a site costing between £7,000 and £8,000 per acre the annual subsidy would be £162 per acre. Payment of this subsidy may be subject to two limitations (*a*) to ensure economic use of the most expensive sites and (*b*) to secure a proper allocation of site costs to housing where the site is used partly for other purposes such as shops or offices.

Part Two

TECHNIQUES

CHAPTER 4

Forms of Dereliction and their Reclamation Potentials
1. Mounds and Spoilheaps

Almost all forms of dereliction can be grouped under two main classifications. Firstly there are the mounds and spoilheaps which rise above ground level and whose reclamation may involve problems of finding filling space. Secondly there are the pits and excavations below ground level, the reclamation of which may involve problems of finding filling material. Where the various types of dereliction are alike in nature and extent or where they may be susceptible to similar methods of treatment they are grouped together below for general consideration of the most effective approach to the problems they pose and in order to suggest the best potential use for the sites after reclamation. . Mounds and spoilheaps are formed in coal mining, quarrying, clay working, the mining of non-ferrous metals and by those manufacturing industries which produce large volumes of waste, such as chemical works, potteries, glass manufactories or steel and iron foundries. Some few mounds have a commercial value and these mounds will be removed by entrepreneurs, contractors or other industrialists requiring the materials contained in the heaps. The remainder can be sub-divided into the groups discussed below.

Colliery Tips, Rucks or Bings (See Plate 13)

When coal is extracted from a seam a proportion of 'dirt' from adjoining strata is unavoidably taken out with it and brought to the surface. This dirt or waste consists largely of coal intermixed with pyrites and stone or shale of a carbonaceous character. It is generally tipped in the vicinity of the colliery in large heaps which may take the form of a conical tip up to 300 feet in height or it may be a high ridge tip in the form of a hogsback, a quarter of a mile or more in length or it may be a low flat tip covering a vast area of land with a comparatively shallow layer of 'dirt'. The shape of the tip varies according to the type of equipment used in forming it, which might be telpherage or aerial ropeways, belt conveyors, Maclane tipping frames, Maison-Bier tippers, tubs and rope haulage, wagons, jubilee trucks, dumpers or lorries.

The high conical tip with a comparatively small base area results from operation of MacLane's dumping frames or telpherage and straight tipping aerial ropeways. The ridge tip arises from use of telpherage, aerial ropeways or wagons which are side tipping. The low flat tip covering a large area of ground is formed by lorries, trucks and dumpers travelling over the top and continually extending the edge. The conical tip has the most unnatural shape and it also has the most persistent bare and desolate appearance. The hogsback tips are frequently on fire but the oldest of them have often weathered and become thinly covered with weeds and coarse grass or scrub. The low flat-topped tips undoubtedly have the least objectionable appearance but they consume land at a much higher rate than the other types.

The dirt produced in a colliery can amount to 20 per cent or 25 per cent of the volume of the coal produced and the total amount of waste tipped into spoilheaps throughout the country is of the order of 40 million tons a year so that, according to the height of tipping allowed, anything from 750 acres to 1,000 acres of land are buried under colliery spoil each year. Horizontal mining and the greater use of coal-cutting machines have increased the proportion of dirt produced and in order to raise production, dirtier seams are being worked, therefore it seems inevitable that the size and number of spoilheaps will increase.

The waste tipped into spoilheaps has a low calorific value— within the range of 2,500 to 5,000 British Thermal Units per lb.

and so the spoilheaps are liable to spontaneous combustion. In the past the forms of tipping most frequently practised were the conical tip and the high ridge tip because aerial ropeways and conveyor systems were found to be the most economical methods of transporting the very large volumes of spoil involved. Both these forms of tip are not only high and unsightly but they are also more liable to take fire. When the Clean Air Act was passed in 1956 there were over 570 spoilheaps burning in England, Wales and Scotland. Section 18 of that Act places an obligation upon the National Coal Board, to take all practicable means of preventing spontaneous combustion in tips and the practical result of this is likely to be the abandonment of high tips and the formation of more low flat tips. These low flat tips are formed in shallow layers by trucks and dumpers; dozers and tracked vehicles are also employed in levelling so that consolidation of the tipped material is effectively carried out and voids and air pockets are avoided. As a result air does not gain access to the combustible material and this type of tip is far less likely to fire.

Where a tip is burning it is advisable to postpone reclamation proposals until the fire has been extinguished or has burnt itself out. If a burning tip must be dealt with, the seat of the fire is copiously doused with water or the burning material has to be dug out and extinguished; either procedure can be most expensive and can take a very long time to complete.

However, when tips have been thoroughly burnt through, they can be quarried for road and footpath material and the fused red ash can be used as ballast or it can be crushed and screened to produce chippings which are suitable for surfacing footpaths, cycle and running tracks, etc. When used as ballast, the ash should be well drained, closely consolidated by rolling and provided with an impervious tarmacadam or bituminous surface when it can form a satisfactory and economical road for carrying light traffic, such as that of a housing estate road. Some screened ballast of large gauge has been used for railway tracks and the material has also provided useful filling in the construction of motor roads. But it must be emphasized that only hard well-burnt ash should be used, and any soft pockets of partially burnt shale must be rigorously excluded because the latter becomes mushy and has no bearing strength under wet conditions.

Those tips which have not been burnt are sometimes composed of a well-weathered and homogeneous shale which is comparatively free from stone, and this may be a suitable material for brick manufacture. There are already a number of brickworks exploiting such spoilheaps and slowly removing them. Other unburnt shale heaps have occasionally provided filling material for large civil engineering projects while a few have been formed into filters for industrial waste liquors and one has even been employed to form the butts for a rifle range. A 200-acre peat bog adjoining the Seafield Colliery in West Lothian has been suggested for reclamation as a regional sports and recreational centre with the high spoilheap graded to form a ski slope using artificial (nylon) 'snow' and equipped with a ski lift. A similar nylon ski run at Torquay is extremely popular and draws patronage from as far as the Midlands.

There are innumerable possibilities, but it has to be recognized that very many mounds are not of saleable material or they may be badly sited for any filling use. Owing to the heavy cost it may be quite impracticable to remove them and there may be no local opportunities for any after-use. However large the tip may be, the value of the comparatively small area of agricultural land it covers is infinitesimal against the removal costs. Such spoilheaps should be given relatively inexpensive cosmetic treatment such as terracing and tree planting or grading and sowing with grass so as to convert them into more pleasant features of the landscape. The methods of carrying this out are discussed in detail in chapter 10.

Oil Shale, Quarry Waste, Clay and Sand Spoilheaps

Oil shale bings are similar to coal tips in general shape, dimensions and the tendency for spontaneous combustion. Where they have been fired, the red ash is usually of a more friable nature than coal shale and pockets of unfired material with a black bituminous binding may remain. However, the surface is less sterile than coal spoilheaps and vegetation becomes established quicker and more easily.

Stone quarries clear the waste from their working areas and generally tip it in conical or ridge-shaped spoilheaps, similar to but smaller than those seen in the coalfields. All the other extractive industries fall into a similar pattern, and as long as working and quarrying continue, these spoilheaps must remain and increase in size. But when working finally ceases, the small and medium-sized heaps can and should be returned to the old workings in almost every instance, provided funds are available to meet the costs of removal. Some of these wastes, such as the softer sandstones, quartzites and limestones become covered with vegetation reasonably quickly, but granite, basalt, slate, mica and the fine sands remain stark and infertile for a very long time.

Occasionally there may be scope for profitably converting some wastes into a useful by-product such as the manufacture of sand-lime bricks or concrete tiles or pre-cast building units. Too little attention is normally given to the commercial utilization of wastes and the manufacture of by-products. In many industries it would seem to be a long-term paying proposition to promote systematic research and special studies into the utilization of wastes on the lines of the research so successfully undertaken into blast furnace slag and referred to on page 77.

When waste heaps are remotely situated or are far from possible markets for the material, such as the waste heaps of the china-clay industry, transport costs may render commercial utilization impracticable, even when a use has been found for the material—in this case the manufacture of Cornish Unit houses.

Where utilization of the waste products is quite impossible the industry concerned could reasonably be expected to set up a sinking fund during the prosperous productive period of the mineral workings in order to meet the costs of returning wastes to the workings when the latter become exhausted. In some cases a very long period must elapse before workings become exhausted and final rehabilitation can be effected. This presents another problem inasmuch as an unsightly spoilheap builds up for generations and in such cases it seems feasible and reasonable to require interim landscaping treatment to be applied. This treatment could be quite simple such as a small amount of terracing covered with topsoil and planted with shrubs, bushes and trees. Similar treatment would also seem applicable to those types of workings which are abandoned for long periods, but final restoration is not undertaken because it is claimed that the workings may be reopened later when commodity prices increase and make further or deeper working profitable, such as is frequently the case in china-clay workings.

Cement, Pottery, Glass and Chemical Wastes

The heavy chemical industry, cement works, potteries, glass manufactories and brickworks generally form low mounds of their wastes and these usually remain stark and bare because the waste material is sterile, or it may even be inimical to plant life. At the same time as the mounds are being formed, excavations for raw materials are being made in the immediate vicinity and when all the minerals have been won, large holes and heaps may be left alongside one another. Very often both the mounds and the excavations could have been avoided by proper planning and programming of the work. It should be incumbent upon these and similar industries to avoid the formation of spoilheaps where excavations are formed within a short distance and it would be reasonable to require these industries to use all future waste for filling the excavations they have made. Throughout the country there are many instances of abandoned excavations and mounds alongside or fairly close to one another.

A few chemical tips containing nitrates, sulphates and phosphates have been quarried for cheap fertilizers and slowly removed but for the most part, the waste products of these industries are of little or no commercial value. Pottery waste and shraff form unsightly tips, and they should not be allowed to be formed above ground level when marlholes are available for filling within reasonable distance.

Dereliction and Reclamation Potentials (1)

Where spoilheaps are being quarried or excavated for the material they contain, a problem occasionally arises because the contractor or entrepreneur with the right of working them, only proceeds very slowly. This may be due to the contractor not having sufficient transport or equipment or there may be a limited demand for the material. Under these conditions, the reclamation can take an inordinate time and the spoilheap may be a jagged eyesore with an accompanying dust or smell nuisance for far too long a period of time. If the contractor is unable or unwilling to step up his rate of working, the local authority should be empowered to arrange for other contractors to share in the work of removal or to require an interim landscaping scheme to be carried out. This landscaping scheme would obviously have to be very modest and most economical because it must be accepted that it might disappear slowly as working progressed. It is certainly worth considering such a temporary landscaping scheme when working may go on for fifteen or twenty years or more.

Ash and Clinker Tips

Ash and clinker is produced by electricity generating stations, gas works, refuse destructors, large boiler plants, etc. Good quality clinker is in some demand for the manufacture of breeze blocks and lightweight walling slabs by building unit manufacturers and municipal authorities, but most of the ash and clinker is tipped to waste, generally in the form of low flat-topped mounds. The power stations alone are currently producing about 6 million tons of pulverized fuel ash a year and this is likely to rise to about 10 million tons a year by 1970. Owing to its physical characteristics, pulverized fuel ash presents many difficulties but there has been some success in finding industrial uses and commercial outlets for the ash in brick manufacture and as an aggregate for lightweight concrete. It is also used as a cement dilutent, as a filler for bituminous products and in the manufacture of building blocks but a very large proportion has to be dumped. The amount now tipped is of the order of 5 million

75

tons a year and this is likely to rise to 7 or 8 million tons a year within a decade. Where the material has to be dumped it can be useful for raising the level of low-lying land which is periodically subject to flooding and it can also be very valuable for filling worked-out gravel pits and other mineral excavations to which it can be pumped in the form of a slurry over a distance of six to eight miles. (See Plates 14 and 15.)

The Central Electricity Generating Board is very conscious of all the problems and has initiated and sponsored a great deal of research to solve them. Investigations have been sponsored at Birmingham and Leeds Universities to ascertain the possibilities of restoring sites that have been tipped upon, to agricultural cultivations. As a surface covering, the extremely light pulverized fuel ash is quite unstable and wind erosion occurs most readily. As a soil it is deficient in some essential nutrients, especially nitrogen and phosphate, while certain elements— notably boron—are present in toxic quantities. As a cultivation medium, the ash retains water satisfactorily and the pH value is high but because the ash is sterile, a balanced microbial quality is not attained for many years. There is a tendency towards cementation and compaction which is liable to form a 'pan' but this can be remedied by deep cultivation.

Where pulverized fuel ash has to be disposed of by dry tipping, there can be considerable and widespread dust nuisance owing to the extreme fineness of the particles, therefore a surface covering of topsoil is essential. Field experiments conducted at Hams Hall generating station by Dr. W. J. Rees of Birmingham University, indicated that after suitable treatment and the application of domestic sewage sludge, the low flat-topped mounds can produce a satisfactory grass ley. Field trials in rotational cropping have been successfully carried out at Connah's Quay generating station by a practical farmer who farms the adjoining land. He was enthusiastically satisfied with his results.

Finding tipping sites for 7 or 8 million tons of ash a year is a massive undertaking and a problem which cannot be satisfactorily solved piecemeal by comparatively small schemes on a largenumber of sites. Such a policy would result in tipping over any agricultural land that could be secured in the vicinity of generating stations. A comprehensive scheme has recently been adopted for disposal of the ash from the Trent Valley generating stations by using it to fill the worked out brick-clay pits near Peterborough. (See Plates 16 and 17.) The ash will be transported by rail in specially designed wagons at the rate of 10,000 tons a day and eventually some 2,000 acres of the old clay workings will be brought back into cultivation. The readiness with which the ash can be pumped as a slurry suggests that this method might be the most economic means of transport and it would seem particularly suitable for a comprehensive back stowage scheme for the coal mines. The enormous quantity of ash which requires disposal opens up large-scale opportunities and even reclamation of the Wash might be envisaged in the long term.

Slagheaps

Slag or scoria produced as the dross or waste in manufacturing iron and steel has usually been side tipped from wagons or trucks to form a long ridge tip. At one time—and not so long ago—it was just another unwanted waste which was difficult to dispose of and the harsh jagged outline of slagheaps rivalled coal tips as discordant features in the landscape. Now it has become a commercially valuable by-product of the iron and steel industry. This promotion has occurred because the uses of slag have been carefully studied and its manufacture is now controlled to give it a chemical composition that is predetermined to meet requirements. As a result almost all furnaces now turn out a product which is free from lime and sulphur and which is often processed by being cast into blocks, crushed, screened and coated with tar or bitumen before it has lost all its furnace heat.

Most of the slag now produced is utilized as road metal owing to its hard wearing qualities and its affinity for tar and bitumen. It is widely used as pitching, graded material and chippings, both dry and coated. It is also used as filter bed media, for walling and as ballast. Foamed slag is another form of this material which has arisen from research and it is in considerable demand for the manufacture of lightweight concrete.

The slag industry is flourishing and it is now an industry in its own right. It stands as a classical example of what can be done in the utilization of wastes and by-products when the problems are intensively studied. From the standpoint of dereliction there should be little further difficulty with slagheaps for they can be quarried profitably and the demand for good slag for highways and other forms of civil engineering construction already exceeds the supply.

However, some of the old tips contain slag which has an excess of lime or sulphur, or slag which is honeycombed or has other defects that render it unsaleable. Such tips have little or no commercial value and they present a hard sterile surface which discourages vegetation. The material in these tips is best used for filling but if there is no construction or excavation in the vicinity which requires filling, then generally the best way to deal with these old slag heaps is to landscape them. This can be done by judicious grading and by introducing pockets of soil here and there in which suitable trees and shrubs can be planted.

Hill and Dale Formations

This is a very common form of dereliction when opencast methods of working have been employed. It can be found at or above ground level as in opencast coal and ironstone workings or it may occur over the floor of a large and deep excavation such as the brickfields where the Oxford Clay formation is being worked in the mass production of 'Fletton' bricks. The hill and dale formation is the result of the method of working where a deep cut or gullet is made to remove overburden and the excavated material is piled on one side. As working progresses a series of parallel cuts and hills are formed. Where a shovel excavator is employed it removes the overburden vertically and mixes the strata. The dragline excavator has a horizontal movement which does not mix the strata and its spreading action usually leaves a more level surface. At whatever level it occurs, the hill and dale type of dereliction can be readily graded and restored for any normal after-use by the employment of heavy earth-moving mechanical equipment.

A great deal of hill and dale dereliction has been reclaimed and redeveloped for housing purposes and industrial uses but most of it has been graded, topsoiled and returned to agriculture by the techniques described later in Chapter 8. Where heavy mechanical equipment is not available, as on a remote site or where there is no intention to redevelop the site or to return it to agricultural use, the cheapest method of dealing with this form of dereliction is to plant it with trees. Planting should take place as soon as possible after the opencast workings cease, so that the tree roots have a chance to establish themselves before the formation becomes consolidated. This ensures better aeration and greater moisture retention and most trees can then be expected to grow at a rate of about two feet a year. There is no need to attempt any partial levelling of the site as the dales or troughs provide good channels for drainage purposes. It is advisable not to plant the bottom five feet on either side of the dales as this provides a track for access when the plantation becomes grown up and it facilitates any extraction of the timber later on.

CHAPTER 5

Forms of Dereliction and their Reclamation Potentials

2. Pits and Excavations

When dereliction takes the form of pits and excavations it has generally been caused by the winning of such minerals as sand, gravel, ironstone, chalk, stone, marls or clays. The dereliction may take the form of a conical pit 300 feet or more in depth, as for example, the Staffordshire marlholes. Or it may take the form of a comparatively shallow excavation only ten or twenty feet deep but spreading over a vast area, as for instance, the Thames valley gravel pits. The depressions arising from mining subsidence can be included in the same classification particularly those which are water filled and known as 'flashes'.

Although these pits and holes in the ground are normally not as conspicuous in the landscape as tips and spoilheaps it is possible that they may eventually present the greater reclamation problem, particularly where there is insufficient material available within reasonable distance to fill them. For instance, filling within the London gravel area amounts to about 70 per cent of the extraction, therefore the gap is continuously increasing because there is not enough waste, refuse and other filling material within economic transport limits. It is difficult to estimate the total amount of filling that may be available on a national scale but it is probably something of the order of 19 million tons per year. There is a potential 11 million tons of house refuse, rubble and miscellaneous wastes and some 8 million tons of fly ash and clinker. At present, filling and reclamation are being done piecemeal and are taking place much too slowly. Good work is being done in many places, but the effective use of all sources of filling requires organization on a national scale.

The various restoration problems of pits and excavations and the purposes for which they might be used after reclamation are discussed below under the three headings of dry pits and excavations; flooded and water-logged workings, including excavations below the water table and subsidence flashes and lastly quarries.

Dry Excavations

As mentioned previously, the form of the dereliction can vary widely and the prevailing local circumstances can differ greatly, consequently the methods of treatment must be flexible and in most cases there should be a choice of alternative methods. Let us first consider the case of the very extensive but shallow excavation in a rural area. The floor of the working is likely to be left in a very rough hill and dale formation of stony subsoil. The probable treatment would involve grading by mechanical equipment and covering with a layer of topsoil. Cultivation could follow quite quickly and the reclaimed working would soon be merged into and be almost indistinguishable from the adjoining agricultural holding but perhaps at a lower level. Where such excavations are in the vicinity of urban areas they can be quite profitably redeveloped at the lower level for almost any urban use such as residential or industrial, and communications and services can be provided to link such development with the adjoining land uses.

When dealing with the deeper but less extensive excavations, it is usually best to fill them to ground level by the controlled tipping of town refuse or by the deposit of industrial wastes and rubble. The larger is the town or urban community the greater is the radius within which filling can be economically carried out. For conurbations, filling near good roads can be a practicable proposition up to a distance of twelve to fifteen miles and in the case of small towns, it is generally feasible up to a radius of four to six miles, but for a village a mile may be the limit.

Where local authorities use domestic refuse for filling excavations 'controlled tipping' methods are generally adopted because they give by far the best results although they entail closer supervision and cost a little more. The term 'controlled tipping' is applied to the system of refuse disposal which was developed at Bradford about half a century ago. The main features of the system are—the refuse must be deposited in layers not exceeding six feet in depth and each layer should be covered with nine inches of soil. Not more than ten square yards should be uncovered at any one time and no refuse should remain uncovered for more than seventy-two hours after deposit. All glass containers must be smashed and all tins must be flattened and placed at the bottom of each layer of refuse. No refuse should be tipped into water. Each layer should be consolidated by the plant running over it before another layer is added. Where circumstances allow, these rules are sometimes modified in respect of thickness of soil cover and area of tip face uncovered but modifications should not be indulged in if they increase the risk of nuisance or provide a less satisfactory surface on completion. Where local authorities have installed composting or pulverizing plant, the product can be used as a filler or it can take the place of topsoil as a covering to the crude refuse. Broken glass used to be a troublesome ingredient in composted refuse but pulverizing plant is now available which is capable of reducing the glass to a fine powder that is almost undetectable.

Within built-up areas, the owner of an excavation can often obtain a good rent for use of the site as a 'shoot' for rubble or as a tip for industrial wastes and refuse. Other owners make a charge for each load tipped. Both methods can be most lucrative for the owners but they may be very unsatisfactory for the local inhabitants, particularly where little control is exercised over the methods of tipping or the type of material tipped. Furthermore, where tipping is by loads, it is inclined to take place very slowly and casually so that the tip or shoot remains an eyesore and something of a nuisance for many years. In these circumstances there is frequently a case for acquisition of the tipping area by the local authority so that the crude tipping can be controlled and programmed to become a proper reclamation scheme. Completion can be hastened by using the shoot for house refuse disposal and where there are several shoots, the tipping can be concentrated on one at a time to complete each in turn instead of having all open over a long period.

Where deep excavations have been filled and it comes to the final surfacing, the best results are obtained by covering with a layer of topsoil twelve inches thick; however, substitutes such as compost, selected or pulverized refuse and sludge from humus tanks of sewage disposal works can be successfully applied. Alternatively the filling material itself can sometimes be treated with soil conditioners and used for covering but this is likely to be more expensive than the importation of topsoil. Finally, the surface is sown with grasses and pioneer vegetation to be gradually brought back to fertility as discussed in detail on page 123 et seq.

The ultimate use of dry excavations after treatment depends very much upon their location and the land uses which are in demand in the vicinity. Large dry excavations within or near urban localities can be absorbed by almost any form of redevelopment for which a need exists. In the countryside, reclaimed sites can be returned to agricultural use, or without any reclamation treatment the sites can be planted with trees at a cost of about £60 an acre. In amenity areas and near popular resorts, abandoned mineral workings can often be readily converted into pleasant and unobtrusive caravan sites at low cost and with little treatment beyond some grading, improvement of access, provision of hardstandings and services and probably a little planting of shrubs and trees. Where the excavation has been caused by mineral workings, it is usual to find that a piped water supply and electricity may have been provided already and hardstandings are often easier to form than on virgin soil. Medium-sized dry excavations in the vicinity of urban localities frequently offer excellent opportunities for conversion into amphitheatres, sports grounds or racing tracks. For these purposes, the floor should be levelled and the sides should be graded or terraced. Small dry excavations can be reclaimed to form excellent playing fields and public open space of all types from an adventure playground for young children to the formal garden or small park.

Flooded Excavations

Most deep excavations are flooded and a large number of the extensive mineral workings which have occurred in river valleys have been taken below the water table. This form of dereliction can vary from a pit with steeply sloping or even almost vertical sides to widespread and comparatively shallow lagoons dotted with islands and surrounded by hummocks of overburden, rejected material and silt from the washing plant. Between these extremes there is scope for a wide range of treatment and the most appropriate to meet local requirements will need to be chosen, but the fundamental principles are that the excavation should be filled to a point above the water level with inert material, and any filling likely to contain organic matter or toxic substances should be avoided in order to safeguard underground water supplies from pollution. The inert filling can include waste from industrial processes or mineral workings, boiler ash, clinker and pulverized fuel ash from electricity generating stations. From a point above water level—usually two to three feet—the filling can be completed by the controlled tipping of refuse and where the redeveloped use of the site calls for a paved surface or hardstanding, this can be provided immediately over the filling. Where a thin grass sward is required for the final surface, carefully graded material can be arranged in the upper layer of filling to facilitate drainage and the whole area can then be covered with topsoil, pulverized compost or a compost of refuse and sludge from settling and detritus tanks, before being sown with grass seed.

Refuse should normally not be tipped into water, but occasionally an impervious substrata may render it feasible where the available supply of innocuous filling material is very limited and the depth of water is not too great. The method evolved in the Egham experiments, entailed division of the excavation into small lagoons, each contained by walls of clinker or similar inert material. Tipping of domestic refuse then proceeded at a rate which ensured that each lagoon was completely filled before the refuse could ferment and cause aerial nuisance by the generation of sulphuretted hydrogen. The use of chromatia bacteria or the injection of compressed air can reduce the risk of smell nuisance and extend the time available for filling each lagoon. Any water undertaking likely to be in the remotest degree affected should, of course, be consulted before any filling method is used which could possibly cause pollution of underground water supplies.

The supply of innocuous filling material is often very limited and in that case it is best used to fill the flooded excavations to a uniform and relatively shallow depth so that the derelict workings become converted into lakes or ponds. Then, depending on their location and extent, they may be most useful as centres for water sports by providing facilities for sailing, water-skiing, skin diving, hydroplane racing, skating or fishing. With any of these uses the verges should be planted with shrubs and trees so that the erstwhile dereliction can serve also as a pleasurable landscape feature. Indeed, whether or not filling material is available, the conversion of flooded excavations into water sports centres should be considered as a possibility wherever there is a demand for recreational facilities within a region.

Subsidence 'flashes' usually call for different treatment. The land surface can be raised above flood level by tipping, but with the subsidence a disruption of drainage almost invariably occurs and a new system of drainage must be incorporated with the filling. Where the subsidence is widespread and gives rise to periodical flooding, the construction of flood banks may be necessary. The 'flashes' frequently extend from the washlands of a river and their filling and reclamation may increase the incidence and duration of flooding elsewhere. Therefore the River Board concerned should be consulted before any remedial or reclamation work is started, so that a mutually beneficial scheme can be designed.

Quarries

Abandoned quarries are not easy things to deal with and it is often difficult to find a use for them. Before they can be used some levelling of the rocky floor is generally essential and this can be accomplished by mechanical equipment in most cases but the judicious use of explosives is occasionally necessary. After re-grading of the floor and suitable spreading or banking of the quarry waste some disused quarries have provided sites for industrial undertakings and others have been converted into storage depots for oil, petrol, explosives and inflammable or dangerous materials. A lot depends upon whether the quarries are below ground level, at or near ground level or whether they bite into a hillside or cut through the crest. Where they are below ground level they can, of course, be filled and reclaimed as described earlier, or they can be adapted to contain the new use at their lower level. Where they are hillside or mountain features they are generally best dealt with as a landscaping problem. Derelict quarries near the coast or within inland amenity areas and national parks or in the vicinity of places of popular resort frequently offer opportunities for ready conversion into attractive, sheltered and unobtrusive camping sites and caravan laagers.

In the lay-out of a disused quarry for conversion into a caravan laager much depends upon the shape of the quarry and the size of caravan to be accommodated, but the Model Standards for Caravan Sites issued in 1960 by the Ministry of Housing and Local Government outline the main design features to be observed. The road framework is a fundamental design feature and the minimum carriageway width should be thirteen feet but this can be reduced to nine feet if a one-way traffic system is operated. Footpaths should be not less than two feet six inches wide. The gross density on any permanent residential caravan site should not exceed twenty caravans to the acre and each caravan should be at least twenty feet removed from every other caravan and ten feet from any roadway. To meet these requirements it is usual to allow each caravan a plot of land of about 1,800 square feet, that is thirty feet frontage by sixty feet depth or forty feet by forty-five feet. Provision should also be made on the site for water supply, drainage, sanitation, ablutions, refuse disposal, fire points, storage space, car parks, hardstandings and a recreational area.

Most quarries take vegetation around their edges fairly quickly and can soon become quite attractive landscape features. Chalk and limestone quarries are generally favourable to vegetation and tree growth and there are numerous examples that are quite charming central features of a splendid panorama, as for example those at Great Doward on the River Wye, when viewed from Symonds Yat on the opposite bank. Igneous rock quarries do not take vegetation easily and they can be dark and very difficult scars in the landscape, like the basalt quarries of Rowley Regis, although where they exhibit bold and jagged features they can make their own contribution in the majesty of a mountainous scene. Quarries can normally be classified according to the rock they produce. The sedimentary group comprising sandstones of all types and conglomerates, limestones (including chalk) and some shales take vegetation fairly readily. The metamorphic group comprising slates, schists, gneisses and some hard shales are difficult to plant. The igneous group comprising granite, diorite, dolerite and basalt are generally barren and inimical to vegetation.

Abandoned Industrial Sites

These commonly comprise ruinous buildings; heavily reinforced concrete foundations for furnaces, boilers and plant generally, tall chimneys, winding frames and gear, railway sidings, quarry screening plant, disused reservoirs, canals, basins, filters, lagoons and every kind of industrial junk and debris that is worthless or has proved expensive or difficult to remove from the site. These abandoned and derelict industrial sites involve no insuperable problems for a competent demolition contractor and most local authorities can cope with them.

Techniques

In many cases they could provide most valuable training for Royal Engineer units in the use of mechanical equipment and excellent practice in the use of explosives and calculation of charges for demolitions. These sites are only cleared when it becomes economical to redevelop them and they may remain eyesores for years.

In all reclamation work the guiding principle should be, to find the most suitable after-use for the derelict land and where waste material is involved, to seek the most profitable uses for it. This entails giving each site individual consideration and it calls for further research into the potential and properties of waste materials.

CHAPTER 6

The Preparation of Reclamation Schemes

Outline of Procedure

Reclaiming derelict land is a type of civil engineering project that is well within the scope and capacity of the municipal engineer's department of almost all local authorities and it can be carried out either by the use of direct labour or in conjunction with public works contractors. Reclamation is generally initiated by a report and recommendation from a landscape architect, town planner or municipal engineer to the local authority. When the authority is satisfied that the proposals are in the public interest and that it can afford to carry out the work, the landscape architect, town planner or municipal engineer is authorized to prepare a reclamation scheme.

Where a scheme is put out to contract the task is usually divisible into four main stages comprising:

(i) A survey of the site and a review of all local conditions which may affect the work followed by preparation of plans and sections which will illustrate the general design and main features of the project. From these drawings a preliminary estimate of the costs can be prepared and at this stage the scheme is usually submitted to the Public Works Committee for detailed consideration. Consultations with the Finance Committee follow and finally the proposals are approved by the Council.

(ii) The landscape architect, town planner or municipal engineer then proceeds with the preparation of all contract

89

documents. These will normally include (*a*) the general conditions of contract; (*b*) a specification describing in detail the works required to be done; (*c*) detailed drawings of the schemes; (*d*) a bill of quantities measuring the amount of work to be done; (*e*) a form of bond and the invitation to tender. When tenders have been returned and one of them has been accepted by the Council the formal approval of the Minister may be necessary before works commence.

(iii) During progress of the works, the landscape architect, town planner or municipal engineer undertake their general supervision and direction to ensure that the specification is being fulfilled in every respect. He will give decisions on any subsidiary problems or difficulties that may arise and he will issue the interim payment certificates.

(iv) On satisfactory completion of the contract, the officer in charge will be concerned with final measurement of all the work done under the contract and with settlement of final cost.

Where reclamation work is carried out by the direct employment of labour and plant there are normally two phases as follows:

(*a*) Survey of the site and a review of all existing circumstances followed by preparation of the plans, sections and detailed drawings, together with a specification, bill of quantities and an estimate of the total cost. These proposals are generally examined by the Public Works Committee and the Finance Committee before being considered by the Council. On acceptance of the proposals by the Council, the project is submitted to the Minister for his approval.

(*b*) When final approval of the scheme is forthcoming the landscape architect, town planner or municipal engineer proceeds to detailed organization of the labour force, plant and transport available and at the same time he prepares time schedules and the programme of work. When

90

these are all put into operation, the officer in charge of the work controls and directs the project dealing with any complications or problems as they may arise and keeping an account of the costs.

Site Investigation and Survey

A preliminary careful reconnaissance is desirable to determine the sequence of work for the site survey and investigation. The time spent on this reconnaissance is amply repaid, for it frequently enables the broad design and programme of reclamation to be envisaged and determined from the onset.

The first objectives of the survey will be to determine the precise boundaries of the site and to plot the various physical features it contains. Normally a series of spot levels are taken and plotted and these should be sufficient to allow of contouring at five-foot vertical intervals. All easements, rights of way and access points must be recorded as well as the exact positions and sizes of all cables, pipes, sewers, overhead lines and other services. Trial holes should invariably be taken out and vertical sections of strata should be prepared. The lengths of haulage necessary between the various excavation areas and filling areas should be measured exactly and recorded. When dealing with deep pools, flooded marlholes or pits excavated below the water table, a careful examination of the geological circumstances may be necessary in order to avoid risks of flooding and subsequent subsidence.

It is advisable to check all site survey data at least once before it is expanded to form the basis of the information which is eventually incorporated into the specification and bill of quantities. The more precisely this is done the greater is the likelihood of avoiding disputes and claims for extras at the final settlement. There is a British Standard Code of Practice, C.P. 2001 (1957)—Site Investigations, which deals with the suitability and characteristics of sites as they affect the design and construction of structures to be erected upon the sites. This code summarizes in a convenient form all the information which is ever likely to be

91

necessary and detailed consideration is given to soil and geological conditions. Standard methods for the taking, examining and testing of soil samples are described. However, the code is really concerned in ensuring the safety of structures which impose heavy ground pressures and all the precautions are not generally applicable in reclamation work; only relevant provisions need be chosen.

Mine Shafts

Old mine shafts and abandoned mine workings which may be partially filled-in or capped are frequently associated with derelict land and these features may not be marked upon the current maps or ordnance survey sheets of the district. Needless to say these hazards can be extremely dangerous if they collapse under heavy equipment. The only hint of their presence might be slight depressions or pock-markings on the surface, or they may sometimes be detected in air photographs, but very often there may be no indication at all beyond a hazy local tradition or impression. If there is any possibility of this danger a search of mining records is essential and a mineral report by a specialist based on the plans of abandoned mines or on the results of efficient boring is desirable.

In 1840 the Geological Survey set up a voluntary Mining Records Office and the Mines Act 1872 made statutory provision for the deposit of plans showing the boundaries of abandoned workings at the Mining Record Office of the Inspectorate Division of the Home Office. Unfortunately, of the vast number of mines worked before 1850 only a few plans are available. Further enactments in 1887, 1896, 1911 and 1954 required additional detail to be shown on the plans of abandoned coal, stratified ironstone, shale and fireclay workings. The position of pillars of unworked minerals and the location of underground faults have had to be shown since 1896; the location of washouts and intrusive dykes since 1911 and variations in level on the boundaries of abandoned works since 1954. These records were consolidated at the Mining Record Office of the Ministry of Power at Buxton and later the National Coal Board became responsible for the safe custody of these plans as agents of the Ministry of Power. In 1931 the Mines Department published a catalogue of plans of abandoned mines and supplements revising the catalogue were published annually until 1938. Further additions to the deposited plans have been recorded by card index held at Divisional Headquarters and at the National Coal Board Headquarters at Hobart House, S.W.1.

Probably the quickest method of obtaining information about abandoned mines is an inquiry to the appropriate Divisional Records Officer of the National Coal Board. The Scottish Division office is at Edinburgh; the Northern Division (Northumberland and Cumberland) is at Newcastle-upon-Tyne; the Durham Division is at Gateshead; the Yorkshire Division is at Doncaster; the North-Western Division is at Manchester; the East Midlands Division is at Nottingham; the West Midlands Division is at Dudley; the South-Western Division is at Cardiff and the South-Eastern Division is at Dover.

The latest plans of working mines, known as the Standard Plans include all known old workings within a certain distance of the districts being worked. As a result of research by National Coal Board surveyors in the different areas of each Division, the presence of some old workings for which there are no plans of abandonments may be indicated on the Standard Mine Plans. Copies of these are maintained at each Area Headquarters and may at least give warning that workings exist even if they do not indicate the actual underground pattern of workings.

Very old shafts (before 1872) may not be recorded and where no plans of abandoned mines are available the site may have to be thoroughly explored for them. Borings to the seam may have to be made to prove the site and since the boreholes should form a regular pattern and not be at random, many boreholes may be required. However, it may be possible, by a geophysical survey of the site, to accurately place a few boreholes and reveal sufficient information to save the expense of further boring. Where old shafts are found (either capped or uncapped) the safest thing to do with them is to fill them solidly to ground level.

When structural development has to be undertaken on a site afflicted with old shafts, exploration work is also necessary to trace the pattern of the old underground workings so that precautions can be taken to guard against collapse and cavitation under loading. For this purpose, boreholes are usually drilled at twenty-foot centres to the base of the seam. Drilling can be carried out with an Atlas Copco B.V.B. 14 waggon drill powered by a compressor of the same make. For core recovery a large rotary core drill with N.X. ($2\frac{1}{2}$ inch diameter) coring equipment has been employed with success, but a more economical method of locating cavities is possible with the pneumatic drilling methods of boring. Hand-held Atlas Copco jackhammer drills with light Swedish steels and tungsten bits are suitable for this purpose and one operator can handle the drill with fifty to eighty feet of rods. Manual operation of the drill enables the operator to feel the jackhammer fall into any cavity and this cannot be established as accurately when the conventional automatic feed waggon mounted pneumatic drill is used. The boreholes are, of course, subsequently used to carry out any necessary back-stowage and for the final grouting.

The Design of Schemes

When all survey data has been accumulated and plotted it becomes possible to proceed with the design of the whole project. It is at this point and on the drawing board that the most economical grading can be worked out and the best design achieved. It cannot be too strongly emphasized that this is usually the critical point in economical design because adjustments at this stage can result in enormous savings. Frequently a very great amount of excavation or filling can be avoided by quite modest variations in the finished levels or in the degree of grading or even by a slight alteration in the phasing of the jobs. In very large projects, it is at this point that computer programmes may have to be prepared.

There are many factors to be given consideration when it comes to the detailed design and in each individual scheme these design factors have to be weighed one against the other because there is infinite variety in local conditions and no two reclamation tasks are exactly alike. Some of the more important factors which may influence a designer in the methods he adopts or the plant he chooses are:

1. The physical, chemical and biological nature of the derelict surface.
2. The extent to which levels vary over the site.
3. The ease or difficulty of drainage.
4. The risk of subsidence or settlement.
5. The means of access available or possible to provide.
6. The haulage distances involved.
7. The availability of filling and topsoil.
8. The likelihood of subterranean fires.
9. Any liability to flooding, waterlogged or marshy conditions in the vicinity.
10. The adjoining land uses.
11. The existence or absence of public services.
12. The purpose or after-use for which the land is to be reclaimed.

There are further factors which, although they may not affect accomplishment of the tasks, can assume outstanding importance because they may have a decisive influence upon the overall financial position and therefore the design must have regard for them. These include such factors as:

1. Location of the site relative to the surrounding use zoning and the types of adjacent development (i.e. whether residential, industrial, etc.).
2. Site values in the district.
3. The urgency for and priority of the reclamation.
4. The resources from which the costs of reclamation can be met.

In a very large project, many or all of the above factors may fall for assessment before the designer arrives at the most favourable method, the most economical and effective organization and the most appropriate equipment and plant. If the ultimate use of the land after reclamation is not already known, it should be decided at the design stage. The most level areas should be reserved for playing fields. For residential and industrial development there should be a uniform fall across the site for economical drainage. Where land is being used for tree planting, landscaping or as a natural park the minimum amount of levelling is required.

Where building development, with an appreciable amount of impervious surfacing, is intended to be provided after reclamation, it is essential at the design stage to calculate the run-off and assess its effects upon the drainage of the whole district. A comprehensive system of sewers and drains can then be provided, to cope with the altered conditions and so avoid any flooding in storm periods.

Plans, Specifications and Quantities

Drawings and documents should be concise but they must give a clear picture of the requirements.

All necessary easements, rights of way and points of access should be negotiated and positively arranged before completion of the contract documents. Where roads, paths or rights of way have to be diverted provision should be made in the specification for their reinstatement to the original or approved alignments. The location of fences and hedgerows should be shown and where they have to be removed an allowance may have to be made for their replacement.

The exact position and sizes of all drains, sewers, mains, pipes, cables and services which might be affected by the works must be shown accurately on the drawings. Drainage possibilities will have been evaluated at the design stage and where necessary a separate detailed drainage scheme prepared; this should be included in the specifications as an integral part of the reclamation proposals. Watercourses are normally reinstated to approved levels and gradients, using impervious material from the site to line them. Existing culverts, drains and ditches may require replacement and may have to be enlarged and regraded to provide adequate capacity for the increased surface run-off.

Trial holes should be excavated so that the soil can be examined *in situ* and if necessary tested. A description of the soil and the soil profile should be given in the specification. When the trial holes have been excavated, it is advisable to leave them open for inspection by contractors during the tendering period.

British Standard Specification No. 1377 (1961) codifies the methods of testing soils for civil engineering purposes. This Standard is divided into four parts, the first of which prescribes the apparatus and methods to be used in the preparation of samples. Part II contains various soil classification tests including determination of—moisture content, liquid limit, plastic limit, specific gravity, particle size distribution and calculation of the plasticity index. Part III deals with chemical tests for determination of—the organic matter content; the sulphate content of the soil and the ground water; the pH value of the soil. Part IV sets out soil compaction tests for determination of the Density/Moisture ratio. Typical data and calculation forms are provided in appendices.

Bills of quantities for reclamation projects can be prepared in conformity with the recommendations of the 'Standard Method of Measurement of Civil Engineering Quantities' published by the Institution of Civil Engineers in 1962. Every item should then be measured in the recognized units and prime cost sums should be restricted as far as possible. Where there is a British Standard Specification for a material it should generally be adopted and its number should be quoted in the Bill against each item covering the material.

When a derelict site is regraded it is generally taken down to levels which allow for respreading of subsoil and topsoil and for its settlement so that the final restored surface will conform with the levels and contours of the adjoining land. Where the site has a covering of topsoil it should be stripped to its maximum depth and stored in dumps apart from the subsoil. This work should be done in dry weather, otherwise damage and waste is caused by the earth-moving equipment. Care is also necessary at this stage to prevent ponding and erosion particularly on

G   97

large sites. Arrangements should be made for adequate disposal of surface water, bearing in mind that there is a larger run-off during restoration than occurs on normally cultivated land. After regrading of the subsoil to predetermined levels, the topsoil is usually spread to a depth of twelve inches. Where the topsoil contains a high proportion of stone and is likely to be cultivated or where a turf surface is required it may be advisable to pass a stone-removing machine over the site at least once in two directions at right angles.

In cut and fill, measurement is generally based upon the amount of cut rather than the amount of fill. Allowances must be made in all calculations for bulking on cut and shrinkage on fill; this may be as much as 25 per cent where heavy mechanical equipment is used. The appropriate allowance varies but it can be determined by simple soil tests. Filling should not be carried out against an existing slope otherwise slipping almost certainly occurs, particularly on a shale face. An allowance should be made for all slopes to be undercut or excavated to form a sheer face. Filling can then be carried out against the sheer face.

Where the work involved cannot be accurately foreseen or where there is a definite risk element—as, for example, in the digging out and extinguishment of a subterranean fire—the item can be billed as a provisional item and paid for as such, upon final measurement. This procedure is generally more equitable and satisfactory than a 'guesstimate' by either party.

In reclamation contracts it is often a very good policy to specify the finished requirements and standards as closely as possible but to allow the contractor reasonable latitude in his methods of attaining those requirements and standards. Where the contractor has been allowed such latitude he has a very strong incentive to work out new techniques and methods or to acquire plant designed especially for the particular job in hand in order to secure a quicker and more economical completion of the contract, to the benefit of all concerned.

In any case, where the work is carried out by an experienced public works contractor the choice of plant can usually be left to him, but the municipal engineer must nevertheless have a general appreciation of the capability of various items of earth-moving equipment.

By far the largest proportion of reclamation work can be classified as light and medium tasks of excavation, filling, levelling or grading. The machines generally employed for these tasks are cable-operated bulldozers or angledozers, tractor-drawn scrapers, graders, scarifiers and rooters of various types.

Heavy clearing, filling or grading necessitates the employment of hydraulically-operated bulldozers, or angledozers, self-propelled scrapers, elevating-graders or loader-excavators and tournapulls. Where heavy excavation or digging is involved, there is likely to be employment for mechanical excavators with shovel, dragline or skimmer attachments.

The haulage of materials in bulk is usually performed by dump waggons, tipping lorries, self-propelled or towed scrapers, conveyor belts or telpherage, railed tubs, jubilee trucks or skip-ways.

Hard formations and soil cementations can be broken up by scarifiers and rooters but where fused slag and rock conditions are encountered it is often necessary to use compressors with drilling and breaking tools or even explosive charges. Any spreading of soil or filling by deposit in uniform layers is accomplished by scrapers of all types or by means of dozers or graders working in team with dump waggons, trucks or lorries. The more precise levelling is generally undertaken by graders. The general characteristics of earth-moving equipment and its more detailed selection for the various tasks presented in reclamation work are discussed later in Chapter 7.

The *General Conditions of Contract, Form of Tender, Agreement and Bond for use in connection with Works of Civil Engineering Construction* agreed between the Institution of Civil Engineers, the Association of Consulting Engineers and the Federation of Civil Engineering Contractors (4th Edition, 1955) is suitable for and can be adapted to meet the requirements and conditions encountered in reclamation schemes.

Techniques

The Regional Survey

Where a regional survey is being undertaken or where the dereliction problems of a county are being reviewed, the approach is somewhat different because the object then is to obtain a comprehensive appreciation of a multitude of diverse tasks and allot priorities to their execution. For this purpose a broader and less detailed survey is required. The essentials are to ascertain the gross acreage of land affected, an approximate estimate of the volume of earth shifting involved, a rough outline of the types of remedial work required and where possible an indication of the purposes for which each site will be used after reclamation and redevelopment.

In a regional survey, a substantial amount of the preliminary work can be accomplished from air photographs but a field survey must follow and the results should be plotted upon six-inch Ordnance Survey sheets. The essential information revealed by the survey should be summarized in a schedule which would accompany the maps. For ease of checking and future reference, the twenty-five-inch Ordnance Survey enclosure numbers and the acreages comprised in each site should be ascertained and included in the schedule. Composite items of such a schedule which was devised for a regional survey within the West Midlands are set out on page 101.

The Appropriate Executive Agency

There has been some debate on the question whether the preparation of reclamation schemes is a task to be shouldered by local authorities or whether reclamation should be a national undertaking. It has been argued that wholesale reclamation might be accomplished more quickly if undertaken on a national basis because very large contracts could be arranged and this would enable more powerful equipment to be devised and brought into use. Alternatively, a direct labour and works organization might be set up, rather on the lines of the original open-cast coal directorate. The protracted negotiations, which

Table VII. Specimen Survey Schedule

Local Authority	Site No.	25" O.S. Ref. and date	Enclosure Nos.	Site Location	Acreage	Outline of Work Required	Suggested use of Site
'W' U.D.C.	123	LXII. 12 Revised 1949	244 250 pt.	Dillaways Lane Moseley Road	2·2 0·8	Filling marlhole approx. 82,000 cu. yds. Pumping and drainage	Residential
'W' U.D.C.	124	LXII. 12 Revised 1949	164 165 pt. 213 214 215 216a	Portobello site Moseley Road	6·8 24·5 5·5	Levelling old pit mounds, approx. 180,000 cu. yds.	Residential and open space
'X' U.D.C.	125	LXII. 5 Revised 1952	254 pt. 262 264	Charles Street Spring Bank	1·5 7·8	Levelling mounds of Chemical waste	Industrial
'Y' C.B.	126	LXII. 11 Revised 1954	321 pt. 321a 321b	Heath Lane	20·3	Levelling pit banks 200,000 cu. yds. Under-ground fires	Residential
'W' U.D.C.	127	LXII. 12 Revised 1949	351	Great Bridge Road	14·71	Filling excavation and surfacing	Community Centre
'X' U.D.C.	128	LXIII. 5 Revised 1952	38 39 65 66 pt.	Stowlawn	14·3	Levelling slag heap and drainage	School site
'Z' B.C.	129	LXXI. 6 Revised 1957	225	Chapel Hill	13·0	Levelling 90,000 cu. yds. Tree Planting	Industry (9) Open Space (4)
'X' U.D.C.	130	LXIII. 5 Revised 1952	135 191 192 193 193a 194 195 212	Bentley Estate	155·3	Levelling. Cut and fill balanced at 370,000 cu. yds.	Residential (116) Open Space (39·3)

frequently delay schemes when works straddle the boundaries of adjoining authorities, would then become unnecessary and the delays associated with applications for loan sanctions and grants would be avoided. A more uniform standard of restoration could be assured, although, of course, this might not be an un-mixed blessing. It has also been argued that the widespread nature of dereliction, throughout the whole country and its heavy incidence in areas which have been exhausted by the contributions they have made to the industrial prosperity of the nation, make the task a moral responsibility of the Central Government.

On the other hand the local conditions and circumstances vary to an extraordinary degree and the local authority is the instrument designed to best cope satisfactorily with these variations, owing to the intimate knowledge it has of the district and its needs. This local knowledge and a vital interest in the effect of dereliction upon the district is not possessed by any other agency. Therefore the local authority seems to be the most favourably placed body to determine how the work shall proceed and to decide the ultimate use of the sites. Furthermore there is, of course, a long tradition that local authorities shall promote all 'town improvements' and undertake any schemes of public benefit which cannot be expected to show financial profits. The finest reclamation that has so far been accomplished has been carried out by local authorities who have been pioneers in every new development in this field. Above all it is most important to foster and maintain a strong civic interest and to promote a local enthusiasm for clearance of all unsightly features from the environment.

Circular 9 issued by the Ministry of Housing and Local Government in 1955 placed upon local planning authorities the onus of preparing surveys and keeping records of dereliction and it also made these authorities responsible for submitting a programme for reclamation. However, the responsibility for carrying out the actual work was left quite open. Local authorities are empowered to do it but they are under no statutory obligation to undertake it.

The Preparation of Reclamation Schemes

In a county borough, the borough council would carry out all the functions of survey, recording, programming and any actual reclamation undertaken but within the administrative county there is usually a division of functions. The county council as local planning authority carries out the survey and does the recording and programming in conjunction with the county district council whether this be a borough, urban or rural district council. Normally the actual work of reclamation is undertaken by the county district council as the local authority concerned.

This division of duties was foreshadowed in a paper presented to the Institution of Municipal Engineers in 1948 when close co-operation between local planning authorities and local authorities was envisaged as outlined in the following extracts. 'In addition to carrying out the survey, the local planning authority might also work out a broad allocation of the uses to which the land could be put after reclamation, in accordance with the land requirements of the area concerned. Having regard for our existing local government organization it certainly appears desirable that the local authority should execute the reclamation work and have a major part in determination of the ultimate use of each site. Upon receipt of the survey particulars and a tentative broad allocation from the local planning authority, it is suggested that the local authority should then make a detailed examination of each site mentioned in the survey and prepare a specific scheme for reclamation of all the derelict land within its administrative boundaries, . . . Local authorities should, of course, combine and work out joint schemes where the circumstances make this advantageous, as for instance, where the volume of earth to be moved is below an economical minimum in one district, or where derelict land overlaps boundaries, or where spoil removal is the task in one district and filling an excavation is the task in an adjoining district. The detailed reclamation schemes could be submitted to the local planning authority for concurrence and consolidation with other schemes before submission for Ministerial approval. In their examination of the schemes, local planning authorities might note any special

103

difficulties and where necessary, arrange to make available financial assistance or specialist advice for the local authority in respect of heavy earth-moving equipment, soil analysis, plant ecology, etc. When approval is eventually forthcoming the local authority would prepare the detailed specifications, bills of quantities, schedules of prices and invite tenders from public works contractors. Alternatively they might elect to do the works by direct labour and submit proposals for the purchase of plant and organization of the work.'

Reclamation problems could also be tackled most successfully by a consortium of local planning authorities and local authorities who might be faced with similar difficulties and circumstances and who might collectively overcome problems which would appear insurmountable to each individual authority. There is room for a number of such consortia who could either work on a regional basis or deal with similar types of reclamation schemes. The consortia would have the advantages of pooled knowledge and resources and could set up a central directing organization which would arrange the programme of work, acquire plant suitable for direct labour schemes and ensure its continuous employment. By this means a standardized procedure for resolving similar problems would be evolved and the directing organization could design special plant and adopt standard components. Alternatively, one or another consortium might prefer to obtain quotations from large contracting firms and enter into joint contracts which would facilitate the employment of heavier equipment and plant. The expenses of the central directing organization could be met by a small levy on the constituent authorities of the consortium in proportion to the value of work executed for each authority. These expenses should amount to less than 1 per cent of the value of the work executed and this would allow for the employment of specialist consultants in engineering, landscape architecture or forestry.

Where derelict land has been well situated and not too costly to reclaim and has been capable of reclamation and redevelopment at a profit, speculators and building contractors have always been prepared to purchase the land and carry out the necessary work. The sites have generally been re-used for industrial or residential development but all this redevelopment has been on a comparatively small scale. Undoubtedly this will still go on, but with the increasing land shortage, there may be the possibility of another type of consortium seeing a likelihood of profit from reclamation on a large scale. Consortia comprising banking, insurance or other financial interests linked with one or more large public works contracting firms and associated with engineering, planning and landscape professional advisers would be capable of operation on a national scale, particularly for redeveloping land in and near urban areas, on similar lines to those now concentrating upon large-scale redevelopment of the central areas and shopping centres of towns and cities up and down the country.

Lea Valley Regional Park Proposals

Since the above paragraphs were written a splendid example of co-ordinated action has emerged in the Lea Valley Regional Park Scheme. The Civic Trust was asked by the seventeen local authorities concerned, to make a study of the Lea Valley and assess its potential for recreational and leisure uses. The Trust's report was published in July 1964 and it contained proposals for the conversion of some 6,000 acres of old gravel workings and waste land into sixteen parks and recreational areas which will stretch from West Ham to Ware—a length of some twenty miles at present occupied by about ten miles of gravel workings, six miles of reservoirs and four miles of predominantly industrial development. The scheme envisages the river and waterways being used for cruising, rowing, water ski and speedboat courses and the land being used to accommodate six golf courses, facilities for all sports with a stadium capable of holding 65,000 spectators, provision of entertainment centres, dance halls, car parks and a wide range of cultural facilities.

Such a conversion scheme for the Lea Valley would present the Metropolis with some 2,500 acres of amenity waters, 1,200 acres of park land, 420 acres of new playing fields, 130 acres for motor sports and 40 acres for botanical gardens. It might cost £30 million but its value in meeting the future leisure demands of North-East London and beyond would be incalculable.

CHAPTER 7

Mechanical Equipment

The work involved in remedying dereliction can be carried out most expeditiously, conveniently and economically by the employment of heavy mechanical equipment. There is a wide variety of this plant available, indeed, one of the outstanding developments of civil and mechanical engineering during the last twenty or thirty years has been the remarkable increase in size and capacity of heavy earth-moving equipment. Plant and machinery can now be obtained which will cope with any reclamation task, however large. The plant in most general use for the work comprises tractors, dozers, scrapers, graders, excavators and load-carrying vehicles. Other plant, such as specially designed locomotives, telpherage or conveyors would probably be brought into much greater use if larger and more comprehensive schemes were undertaken. The following brief notes describe each type of equipment and give a general appreciation of the characteristics and capabilities of the various units.

Tractors

Tracked vehicles are essential for work on soft ground of low-bearing capacity or where the going is very rough and uneven. Tractors are the forbears of all earth-moving equipment inasmuch as they first linked the immense power of the diesel engine with the advantage of uniform load distribution over tracks. The machines are of very robust construction to withstand heavy stresses and rough treatment and all bearings are specially sealed to keep out grit, mud, etc.

The tracks are assemblies of flat steel plates, each having a rib or grouser. The large area of the track ensures that the track pressure on soft ground does not exceed eight pounds per square inch while a large grouser area enables the maximum drawbar pull to be attained.

The power of a machine normally ranges from 25 horsepower to 400 horsepower and it is important to use tractors and equipment that match one another. Tracked vehicles are not generally suitable for long hauls. If tractors have to be used for such tasks, rubber-tyred wheeled types are available.

Bulldozer (See Plate 18)

The bulldozer attachment of a tractor consists of a hollowed scoop-like blade which is fixed to the front of a tractor by means of a cable or hydraulically operated steel framework that controls movements of the blade in a vertical plane. The blade is pushed in front of the tractor and owing to its prominent lower edge and curved back, a rolling motion is given to the soil, which is cut and becomes piled up ahead of the blade. Thus a large quantity of soil can be driven forward in front of the machine particularly when an operator avoids sidespill of the soil by working downwards within excavation lanes. When the blade is slightly raised, spoil may be spilled fairly evenly under its lower edge and spread over the length of travel. A bulldozer is comparatively easy to operate and it is the best tool to use when a large amount of spoil has to be pushed fifty to a hundred yards. The finished surface will not be quite level and to produce reasonable level finishes over any distance requires a very skilled operator. Even then the results obtained by a bulldozer are inferior to those more easily attained by a grader.

Angledozer (See Plate 19)

This attachment is similar to the bulldozer except that the

blade can be adjusted in height and set at an angle (usually 30 deg.) to the travelling axis of the tractor; the blade is generally longer than that of the bulldozer. The angledozer leaves spoil in the form of a windrow and the equipment is useful for spreading or for backfilling excavations such as trenches. It can also be used for cutting out flat formations or terraces on the side of slopes. The blade can be tilted down at the trailing edge or at the leading edge when it can be used for starting cuts on a side slope or for forming a camber or crossfall.

Dozers Generally

Dozing attachments equipped for cable operation rely entirely upon the weight of the blade to maintain cutting level and in very hard ground the blade may be forced out of position giving an irregular formation floor. The hydraulically-operated dozer is not forced out of position by hard ground and in fact a downward force can be exerted which is occasionally of great value.

An angledozer can, of course, be adjusted to work as a bulldozer but a bulldozer is rigid and cannot be angled. The performance figures of dozers vary widely according to the working conditions, but in favourable circumstances a D.8 angledozer should move 300 cubic yards of hard earth in a day's work. Bulldozer performance will be slightly less but the earth may be moved over a longer distance. In broken rock, using a ripper with D.8 angledozer, up to 200 cubic yards of spoil can be moved in a day. Dozers are available in various stock sizes from a D.4 of 43 horsepower and weighing five tons to a D.8 of 130 horsepower weighing fifteen tons. However, if soil has to be moved more than 100 yards it is usually more economical to pick it up with a scraper or dumper and carry it away rather than to push it with a dozer.

Where filling, levelling or grading has been done by heavy tracked mechanical equipment there is a high degree of consolidation which renders unnecessary a long period for settlement before redevelopment is undertaken or the site is put to its new use. This is because the blade of the machine spreads the material fairly evenly in relatively thin layers and then the tracks of the vehicles exert a uniform pressure which ensures thorough compaction of each layer before the next is added.

Scrapers (See Plate 20)

These are self-loading machines generally hauled by tractors and cable operated. A scraper is the best tool for any task where earth has to be excavated for a shallow formation and hauled a distance of up to 400 yards.

The carrying bucket or bowl is slung between two axles and fitted with a cutting edge of curved offset design which facilitates penetration of all types of soils and keeps the earth flowing in to the centre of the bowl with a 'boiling' action. A moveable apron can be lowered over the cutting edge to prevent soil escaping while it is being hauled away. The back is not attached to the bottom or sides and may be moved forward by its control cables so that the spoil can be ejected over the cutting edge while the scraper is moving, thus the load can be spread evenly as it is discharged. The machine is normally fitted with large pneumatic tyres so that it can work in soft ground. The capacities of scrapers range from four to forty cubic yards. A sixteen cubic yard scraper on a round trip of half a mile will move about 66 cubic yards an hour. The large 225 horsepower Tournapull in conjunction with a 300 horsepower Tournadozer will move 300 cubic yards a minute. For long hauls and heavy clearing large self-propelled scrapers are generally used. (See Plate 21).

Motor Grader or Auto-Patrol (See Plate 22)

The grader is driven by a diesel engine fitted to the rear of the frame and it is equipped with a tandem drive and oscillating tandem wheels. The frame is very strong with a raised central portion from which is suspended a turntable that has the grading blade fixed beneath it. The blade turntable may be racked outwards on either side and set at any angle to suit the cutting resistance and the power of the engine. The twelve-foot blade

110

presents a concave surface to the work so that the soil is scooped up and rolled in front of it. Owing to the set of the blade, the soil works down to the trailing edge and is discharged as a side ridge. The grader will operate forward or in reverse and the front wheels can be made to lean either way. Forward working in long stretches is the most efficient use. The grader can be a difficult machine to control and requires a highly-skilled operator if full use is to be made of it.

Elevating—Grader (See Plate 23)

This tractor-drawn machine cuts the earth and lifts it into a lorry or dumper. The cutting blade can excavate to a width of nine feet six inches and to a depth of two feet in soft material; an average cut is four feet wide by eighteen inches deep. The machine can grade uneven contours and leaves a smooth cut surface. The spoil slides on to a moving belt which is driven by a 150-horsepower diesel engine and the machine has a maximum loading capacity into wagons of a ton per second. This speed necessitates the employment of a fleet of large dump wagons or lorries. A suitably balanced team of tractor, loader-excavator and large dumpers can move 500–700 tons per hour.

Excavator—Loader (See Plate 24)

Basically, these are tractors equipped with a bucket or shovel which is capable of being raised or lowered and which is fitted with a cutting edge. The machine can be driven forward with the shovel lowered so that the cutting edge excavates the soil until the shovel is filled. The shovel is then lifted and carried to the dump waggon, into which the spoil is discharged. The machine is available in a wide variety of types and sizes up to a bucket capacity of 24 cubic yards. The smaller wheeled types are often known as Front End Loaders and the tracked vehicles are known as Traxcavators. The bucket can be equipped with teeth and it is sometimes designed for bottom or sideways discharge.

Techniques

Universal Excavators (See Plates 25, 26 and 27)

These machines consist of a driving cab with the controls, engine and operating winches mounted on a heavy frame which can be made to turn a full circle on a tracked chassis. Various excavating equipments can be attached to the frame so as to form a shovel excavator or a dragline excavator or other tool according to the task and these will all excavate in a full circle around the machine.

The shovel attachment consists of a jib to which is pivoted a shovel arm and shovel. In excavating, the shovel arm is forced upwards and forward into the 'face' of the material and all its work is done above track level. There are various patterns; in one type the shovel is forced into the face by means of operating cables which cause the arm to slide forward (relative to the jib) at the pivot; in another type the shovel is attached to the jib and is forced into the face by the weight of the jib. The height of the working face should be at least four feet to allow of the bucket being filled in one upward sweep. The Lima shovel is claimed to be capable of stripping 1,500 tons of hard ground or soft rock in twelve hours.

The dragline attachment consists of a long jib with a bucket supported and controlled by steel cables. The bucket may be dropped at any point around the machine within the radius of the jib and is filled by drawing it towards the machine. The contents of the bucket may be discharged into dumpers or swung around and deposited thirty to 200 feet away. The dragline excavates below its track level. The best angle for the jib is between 30 deg. and 37 deg.

The skimmer attachment consists of a boom and a shovel which slides along it for filling. Excavation is above track level and it can be done with reasonable accuracy. Shovels or buckets are generally armed with teeth or tynes along the cutting edge to facilitate penetration. The face shovel, grab (clamshell), backacter and trencher assemblies are not often suitable for reclamation work.

112

Plate 18. Euclid. T.C. 12. Crawler tractor with twin engines developing 425 h.p. fitted with cable operated bulldozer. Ironstone workings, Corby, Northamptonshire

Plate 19. Challenger crawler tractor fitted with angledozer

Plate 20. Euclid. T.C. 14. All wheel drive motor scraper. Capacity 14 cubic yards (struck) to 20 cubic yards (heaped). Twin diesel engines (front and rear), each of 148 h.p. China clay workings, St. Austell, Cornwall in background

Plate 21. R. G. Le Tourneau self-loading electric digger. Powered by two 475 h.p. diesel engines coupled to A.C. and D.C. generators with electric motors at all points of power application, including a D.C. motor in each wheel. Capable of self-loading at the rate of one ton per second

Plate 22. Aveling-Barford 99H. motor grader with 15 h.p. diesel engine. Independent drive and steering to each wheel. Hydraulic blade manipulation allows for a banking angle up to 90 deg.

Plate 23. The elevating-grader

Plate 24. R. G. Le Tourneau rubber tyred electric excavator with articulated steering. Bucket capacity from 16 to 24 cubic yards

Plate 25. N.C.K.—Rapier. Face shovel with $3\frac{1}{2}$ cubic yard bucket. For heavy duty digging and loading

Plate 26. N.C.K.—Rapier. Dragline with 60-foot boom and 1¾ cubic yard bucket

Plate 27. A small skimmer excavator

Plate 28. Euclid. R. 45. Rear dump lorry Payload 45 tons. Capacity 30 cubic yards (struck) to 36 cubic yards (heaped). 530 h.p. diesel engine. Twin three-stage double acting hoist jacks for tipping

Plate 29. Twin tine heavy duty ripper fitted to rear of wheeled tractor

Plate 30. Sheepsfoot Vibroll. Weighs 5¼ tons and is usually tractor hauled. A 52 h.p. diesel engine, mounted at the rear, operates the Vibrator gear housed within the roll

Plate 31. A rotavator that can be attached to any three-point linkage tractor up to 60 h.p. It gives a depth of cut up to 8 inches and a tillage width of 70 inches

Plate 32. Tree transplanting machine. The scoop or shovel-blade has dug out the root ball and the mature tree has been lifted and is being transported to its new location. A pioneering experiment by the National Coal Board at Shortwood open-cast site, Trowell, Nottinghamshire

Plate 33. Shale planer in one of the deep Lower Oxford claypits at King's Dyke Whittlesea

Transportation (See Plate 28)

Where a large amount of spoil has to be moved a considerable distance it can be economical to use steam locomotives and steel tipping waggons on light railway track. But most reclamation tasks involve short hauls and comparatively high tonnages; in such circumstances removal by earth-moving mechanical equipment, such as dumpers and scrapers, is cheaper and more flexible. Furthermore, the scrapers can build, consolidate and extend the tipping areas if necessary without the employment of bulldozers or other spreading equipment. Heavy dumpers give good consolidation and reduce the risks of fire, where the spoil is liable to spontaneous combustion. Very powerful dump vehicles are available with engines of over 500 h.p., massive frames and strong steel bodies, which are capable of transporting 45 tons or 30 struck cubic yards (36 cubic yards heaped) per trip. Rear-tipping dump wagons are in general use but side-tipping vehicles are employed for some tasks.

Aerial Ropeways and Belt Conveyors

When very large volumes of material have to be taken over obstacles or have to negotiate steep gradients, aerial ropeways may be employed. They are seldom affected by adverse weathes conditions except high cross-winds, but they involve the erection of semi-permanent tower structures and are not flexible. They also necessitate the use of spreaders such as dragline, scraper, bulldozer or calfdozer.

Conveyors on the other hand are usually flexible and easily extended but they can be seriously affected by weather conditions. The freezing of idlers may result in broken belting; cross-winds tend to lift the belt and lubricants freeze unless the belt is kept moving. Enclosure of the belt in a tunnel of corrugated steel sheeting is the expedient usually adopted to overcome these difficulties but this decreases flexibility and increases costs. With every form of belt conveyor it is essential to make pro-

H   113

vision for spreading the spoil and for this purpose a swivel-head conveyor may be used in conjunction with a bulldozer or dragline.

Auxiliary Equipment

Many other forms of equipment find some occasional use in reclamation work and most of them are either pushed, pulled or powered by tractors. These comprise such plant as rippers, sheepsfoot and other rollers, traxcavator shovels and backfillers, blade graders, rotavators, gyrotillers and harrows.

The ripper is a heavy machine with a strong steel frame mounted on a single axle and fitted with three or five tines having specially hardened and replaceable steel tips. Towed by D.8 tractors the rooters penetrate and break up hard ground in preparation for excavation by scrapers and dozers. Generally they are a more speedy alternative than loosening the surface by compressor tools. (See Plate 29.)

Sheepsfoot and other rollers are towed behind tractors and are usually used to consolidate filled areas, particularly where no heavy-tracked vehicles are employed on a job. (See Plate 30.)

The blade grader is also towed by a tractor and it performs a similar function to the autopatrol, but it is only suitable for the lighter tasks. Both front and rear wheels are equipped for leaning and the tractor-pole is steerable.

The Rotavator is a rotary tilling machine which is much more efficient than the plough in breaking up the soil and soilpans, and it has the advantage of a gearbox that gives the rotor blades a variety of speeds, so that the machine is capable of being used under almost every soil condition. The rotavator is drawn by a tractor and powered from the tractor drive take-off through a sliding universal drive shaft to the gearbox and thence power is transmitted to the blades by a chain drive with a shock absorber device interposed to protect the machine from damage if the blades strike a fixed object. Blades are mounted on the rotor so that they only enter the soil one at a time and the depth of penetration can be adjusted. A trailing or rear soil shield can be lowered to control the flow of soil through the rotor and so regulate the fineness of the tilth produced.

The rotavator is particularly useful in breaking up and completely mixing the soil with fertilizers, soil conditioners, seeds, manure or surface vegetation to form an even depth of tillage and a good seedbed. Two or three passes of the machine set to a depth of three or four inches will quickly create a reasonable surface or a seedbed. The second pass is generally made at right angles to the first. (See Plate 31)

The gyrotiller is a tracked vehicle driven by a diesel engine. Two sets of heavy tines are set around circular steel bands which rotate in opposite directions, digging into and churning up heavy soil to form a loose cultivable surface, the depth of which can be regulated.

Harrows are used for breaking down lumpy soil before grading. Disc harrows are the type more generally employed. Chain harrows are effective in forming a fine top tilth to receive the seed and for covering it.

Transplanting Machines (See Plate 32)

Mechanical equipment has been designed for the lifting and immediate replanting of large semi-mature trees and hedges. It consists of a 220 horsepower rubber-tyred Michigan tractor with four-wheel drive fitted with a scoop which digs deep enough to lift the tree without damaging the roots. The scoop is a hydraulically-operated shovel blade whose angle of penetration can be varied. A cone-shaped hole up to six feet deep and slightly larger than the root-ball of the tree to be moved is dug by the transplanter where the planting is required. The machine then digs out the tree to be moved by a series of cuts so as to form a firm root-ball. If access is restricted it is not essential to cut around the tree as one cut can be sufficient to move a moderately-sized tree. The tree is then lifted out and cradled in the transplanter's bucket for removal to the new site. Where the tree has to be carried a considerable distance involving a journey by road, a special self-loading trailer is used. The trailer is shaped to accommodate the tree without the necessity of wrapping the root-ball. Even the more tender fibrous roots can be removed undamaged but it is important to replant as quickly as possible to ensure that the roots do not suffer from exposure. The mechanical transplanter deposits the tree in the previously prepared hole and the soil is packed and tamped firmly around the roots by a small mechanical shovel. The refilled area is copiously watered to prevent the formation of airpockets and to hasten settlement of the soil. Guys are seldom required to hold the tree in its new position. In some cases the use of a plastic spray may be advised on some or all of the foliage in order to reduce transpiration losses during the period immediately after transplanting.

Equipment can be obtained which will transplant trees up to sixty feet in height and a trunk diameter of nineteen inches. The costs of mechanically transplanting a tree over about half a mile amount to about £5 or £6 as against at least £50 when carried out by manual labour and a planting rate of one tree per hour can normally be attained.

Hydraulic Sluicing

Where an ample supply of water is available and large quantities of material have to be excavated on a confined or congested site and where the spoil may have to be conveyed some distance with an available fall, it is worth investigating the possibilities of hydraulic sluicing. In this method, heavy duty pumps discharge water through large nozzles (two inch to eight inch diameter) which direct high-velocity streams of water against the earth or spoil at pressures of between 100 and 500 feet head. The water carries away about 10 per cent of its volume in solids, along a graded run-off system, especially designed to avoid sedimentation and discharging at rates of from two to sixty cusecs.

Explosives

Occasionally compressor tools and explosives may be necessary to loosen compacted or rocky material in order to ease the

116

excavation work. Gelignite, ammonal or blasting powder are the explosives most likely to be used. Gelignite is a good general explosive suitable for shot-firing in dry or wet holes. The 'low freezing' variety should be used in cold weather. Ammonal or blasting powder is more suitable where a lifting force rather than a heavy shattering force is required. Initiation is usually by electrical detonators and exploders, but sometimes safety fuse burning at the rate of two feet per second is more convenient. Although only an elementary knowledge of explosives and the preparation of charges is necessary, the work should be under the supervision of an experienced quarryman or a qualified engineer. Where the work is widespread or a large number of charges are involved the explosives manufacturers should be consulted; they are only too ready to co-operate and to send an experienced representative to advise on the best methods to be adopted.

Plant Adaptation

Perhaps the point which requires most emphasis is that heavy mechanical equipment is already available or can be devised to cope with the largest reclamation task. The draining of Black Lake in Quebec affords an interesting example of large-scale earth-moving organization. The lake covers an area of more than 500 acres and overlays asbestos deposits which would last a mining company forty years. So the company has undertaken drainage of the lake and the dredging of some 37 million cubic yards of overburden.

The dredger which weighed 200 tons was brought up in eleven sections and it is capable of moving a bank of over-burden 250 feet by thirty feet by eight feet in forty minutes. It uses a rotary cutter seven feet in diameter on the end of a boom and is powered by an electrically-driven 800 horsepower motor at 24 r.p.m. The cut material is removed hydraulically by a ten-foot diameter suction pump of 6,000 horsepower and carried to a deposition area by a thirty-two-inch diameter steel pipe with the assistance of other booster pumps.

Techniques

The provision of reclamation equipment of this dimension is unlikely unless work is carried out on a national scale, because there is not the profit incentive, but it illustrates the possibilities. All equipment is designed initially for profitable industrial purposes but the same designs meet reclamation needs. One of the largest single reclamation tasks carried out in this country was the conversion in 1961 of a derelict colliery site of some 320 acres at Tinsley Park, Sheffield, to accommodate a new steel mill for the English Steel Corporation. The work included removal of a colliery spoilheap and levelling a waterlogged area. Over 3 million cubic yards of spoil were excavated and moved in 150 working days and this involved an average one-way haul over half a mile of some 20,000 cubic yards per day. The main instruments were 24 cubic yard and 18 cubic yard motor scrapers, excavators, graders and a fleet of rear dump trucks. Some 200,000 cubic yards of rock were encountered and this was broken up by tractors with hydraulically-operated rippers, before loading by the scrapers.

Each industry gives rise to different types of dereliction and the form of the dereliction may vary within an industry from one locality to another. Therefore there is infinite scope for ingenuity and improvisation in the selection and adaptation of plant to secure economical restoration.

In all future mineral working it cannot be too strongly emphasized that where restoration is planned before dereliction occurs, it can be arranged much more economically and frequently the two processes of winning and reclamation can be accomplished by the same plant and can merge into a single continuous process.

Possibilities of New Techniques and Procedures

New and more efficient plant and techniques are bound to be developed continuously, particularly when reclamation is undertaken on a large scale and if contractors are allowed maximum latitude in the choice of methods to be adopted to secure a specified result. The finished requirements and standards should

118

be clearly and closely specified but in such work as reclamation there is a decided advantage in giving the contractor as much freedom as possible in his methods of attaining the requirements and fulfilling the specification.

A good example of plant designed for a specific task is the Shale Planer used for digging brick clay from an eighty-foot working face in the Isle of Ely (see Plate 33). The clay is sliced from the face by an endless band of large steel chisels and drops on to a conveyor belt (which can be seen on the pit floor) which loads it into trucks for transporting to the grinding mill.

Given an assured demand for very large or specialized plant, there is plenty of native inventive genius in this country to design and provide such plant. For example, there are many parts of our coalfields where large shale tips are to be found fairly close to deep marl holes and again in Cornwall, the deep excavations of china-clay workings generally have their huge waste tips of silica sand alongside. When such reclamation tasks are tackled piecemeal and on a small scale they frequently cannot be done in the most economical manner because the heaps and holes are just too far apart for normal earthmoving equipment to operate cheaply and to its best advantage. Consequently the spoil may have to be hauled in lorries and this inflates the contract price. With reclamation organized on a national scale all dereliction of this type could be programmed for reclamation, giving an assurance of continuous employment, and this would encourage the design of special equipment to deal with the circumstances and cope with the requirements in the most economical way. There are many forms of dereliction for which a combination of coal-cutting machinery and portable telpherage would seem with modifications to be an appropriate development. There are other cases where mechanical excavators and extended conveyor belts might be adapted to give the best results. Where hydraulic sluicing proved to be the best procedure, improved and more powerful portable pumps with closed run-off systems could be devised to cope with larger tasks as has been done already in America. It is rarely worth while producing such special plant for single tasks undertaken at long intervals but where there are large numbers of similar tasks undertaken continuously, the extra costs of specially designed plant can soon be written off.

CHAPTER 8

Surface Restoration and Pioneer Vegetation

After a derelict site has been filled, levelled or graded there remains the problem of surface restoration or of providing a new form of surface suitable for the ultimate use of the site after redevelopment. The intensity of the problem depends upon the chemical, physical and biological nature of the graded material or filling and upon the type of after-use proposed for the site.

Where the site is to be used for industrial redevelopment there may be no problem, because most of the surface is likely either to be covered buildings with or provided with an impervious paving. Apart from the area covered by factory buildings, much of the site is likely to be required for storage or warehousing purposes to accommodate raw materials, manufactured products, packaging, stock and spares for plant, while a great deal of the remainder of the site might well be used for the loading, unloading, servicing and parking of vehicles. (See plate 34.)

When the site has to be redeveloped for residential purposes, or for shopping and business uses or to accommodate schools, colleges or public buildings, the areas which are built upon, paved or used for roads are again unlikely to be troublesome, but in these cases an appreciable proportion of the site may be required for gardens, playing fields, grass verges or open space of some sort and then a degree of fertility may have to be created in unpromising or even sterile soil.

Where it is proposed to utilize the reclaimed site for agriculture, for smallholdings or allotments, large playing fields or open spaces the problems of raising the fertility level of the soil can become paramount as well as difficult and expensive.

Filled sites

The method of filling a site that has to be built upon should be related to the anticipated loading to be borne by the site after redevelopment, especially where such loading is likely to be concentrated upon a relatively small area. The employment of heavy tracked equipment enables a high degree of consolidation to be attained, and within limits, it is often possible to design the consolidation to meet the loading requirements without any subsequent subsidence or settlement. But there is the other extreme—when deep filling has taken place without any precautions of compaction in shallow layers—and then a considerable amount of settlement can be expected, particularly if the tipped material has contained tins, cans, organic substances or ungraded waste, giving rise to voids or arching and subsequently to subsidence and collapse.

Unless the method of filling or degree of consolidation is known, it is prudent to allow a long period of settlement for filled sites and to avoid any concentrated loading such as retort bases or foundations for heavy plant. If constructional work under such conditions is quite unavoidable, it will be necessary to resort to the use of piling and the provision of heavily reinforced grillages and concrete rafts in order to distribute and sustain the loads. Furthermore, where the site has been tipped with chemical wastes, slag, ash, etc., there may be sulphates or other acid compounds present in or near the surface which could attack and disintegrate concrete structures or foundations. In such cases, soil tests and analyses are essential before any buildings or services are designed. These soil analyses will indicate the treatment necessary to overcome the disability. Occasionally light contamination can be neutralized or it can sometimes be blanketed by a layer of soil or inert filling material, but heavily polluted soil may have to be dug out and replaced by innocuous material.

Surface Restoration and Pioneer Vegetation

The Restoration of Fertility

A great deal of derelict land should be returned to agricultural uses and restored eventually to normal fertility levels. A large amount will also have to be landscaped or given amenity treatment and for these purposes it will be necessary to establish plant life and restore some measure of fertility. These tasks are not generally difficult where reasonable drainage and an adequate covering of good topsoil can be provided. Unfortunately, there is always a scarcity of good topsoil and in many cases it may be necessary to adopt a special restorative treatment in order to improve the soil environment and establish pioneer vegetation in whatever material happens to be available on the site.

The conditions prevailing at each site will determine the appropriate treatment and a careful survey of these conditions should be made. The care taken in this survey will be well repaid in achievement of more rapid restoration. Firstly, the existing soil structure should be examined and its nutrient or toxic status should be ascertained. The species which flourish in the vicinity and the stage of succession reached by any existing vegetation on the site should be observed as well as the plants which do well in the wider neighbourhood. Drainage conditions, elevation, degree of wind exposure and the extent of atmospheric pollution are all factors which may have a profound effect and they must be taken into account.

The surface of a derelict site frequently varies from sterile shale or heavy clay to a fine ash that may be toxic or inimical to growth of vegetation. In improving the soil environment, the immediate objective is to build up at least two or three inches of 'live' topsoil, that is a topsoil which has the optimum crumb-structure and biological activity that promotes root development. This is normally accomplished by mulching or the application of heavy dressings of any kind of organic matter and ploughing or discing these dressings into the surface. The best-known organic matter is well-rotted animal or farmyard manure, but there have been

123

successful applications of other wastes, such as the sludge, detritus and humus from domestic sewage disposal works; nightsoil; streetsweepings and gulley sludge; river, canal and estuarial dredgings; brewery waste and waste soil from beet sugar factories. Sewage disposal works dealing with wastes from industrial areas may produce sludges and humus contaminated with toxic metals such as zinc or copper, which may render them unsuitable for use.

Earthworm Inoculation

When mineral workings cease or where spoil and wastes have been deposited on a site, the fertile soil structure is frequently destroyed and there is usually a difficulty in obtaining adequate and uniform surface drainage, resulting in ponding on level areas and erosion on slopes. This may be due to the presence of subsoil on the surface, or to too dense a compaction, or the formation of a pan, or to an absence of soil animals and bacteria owing to excessive acidity of the environment. Before the site was disturbed, it probably had a high moisture capacity and to a great extent, uniform drainage occurred through the granular texture of the soil and the burrows and tunnels made by soil animals, particularly earthworms.

As Charles Darwin demonstrated in his classic study on *The Formation of Vegetable Mould Through the Action of Earthworms*, published in 1881, the common earthworm creates topsoil. Earthworms generally live in the upper eighteen inches of the soil profile and they ceaselessly eat their way through the soil, devouring it, together with rotting vegetation, dead organic matter, garbage and litter of all sorts. Occasionally they burrow deeper into the subsoil and bring up new mineral material. All this passes through the digestive mill of their alimentary canal and is subjected to the digestive secretions and then finally ejected as a finely comminuted and colloidal, soluble humus which is a natural plant fertilizer and a perfect topsoil.

In this country, there are about twenty-five species of earthworm and some ten varieties or sub-species. It has been estimated that at a concentration of 25,000 to 50,000 per acre, earthworms can produce ten to eighteen tons of castings per year. A density of fifty per square yard, that is, a rate of 250,000 per acre is not unusual in favourable soil of slightly alkaline reaction. The density of earthworm population can be readily increased by spreading compost, animal manures and vegetable litter over the surface. Colonization of a site from adjoining land can also be effected in this way.

Although earthworms subsist in a very wide range of latitudes and soil conditions, both young and mature worms may not survive when transposed to a new location, but earthworms will generally adapt themselves to the nutritional environment into which they have been hatched. Therefore they are best propagated by scattering egg-capsules over the surface of the site and lightly raking them in or covering with a thin layer of soil or compost. The egg-capsules have an incubation period of two to three weeks according to temperature and moisture conditions. Hatched from the egg-capsule as fully fledged, the earthworm immediately begins its life work of devouring, honeycombing and cultivating the surrounding soil in search of sustenance and incidentally facilitating aeration, water absorption, root penetration and drainage. The young worm develops rapidly to reach the reproductive stage in sixty to ninety days.

Egg-capsules are obtainable commercially or from an entomology research station. Inoculation of a site with earthworms is best done in spring or early autumn when temperatures are relatively high and humidity and soil moisture are likely to be favourable. Before earthworm inoculation is undertaken, it is advisable to dig a pit on the site (preferably during the summer months) so that the soil profile can be examined down to the unaltered geological parent material. It will then be possible to ascertain the amount and depth of any existing or former earthworm burrows, the development and depth of plant rooting and the degree of acidity or alkalinity at the different horizons. If hydraulic seeding is carried out on the site (as described on page 139) the egg-capsules can be very conveniently sprayed over the area mixed with the seed and fertilizers in the form of a slurry.

They are then covered with the straw mulch which ensures an even ground temperature and induces rapid germination.

If advice is required on the species of earthworm likely to be most successful, an entomologist should be consulted. The National Agricultural Advisory Service, Entomology Department at Shardlow, Derbyshire, has advised on problems in open-cast coal sites and ironstone workings. Other similar research has been carried out at Rothamsted Experimental Station, Harpenden, Hertfordshire, and at certain Universities.

Topsoiling

Where possible, the top few layers of filling should be of carefully selected and graded material and an adequate drainage system for the whole site should be incorporated into these upper layers. To ensure that there is no waterlogging or ponding, subsoil clay and stony material should be avoided as far as is practicable. The final surface covering of imported topsoil is then spread to an even thickness. For satisfactory cultivation, filling and topsoiling should be carried at least two feet above the permanent water table. When topsoil has been removed and stored—as in the working of surface minerals—it often deteriorates, particularly if stored in bulk for too long a period. However, it soon recovers its fertility when respread and given a little careful treatment. Where surface mineral workings are commenced within reasonable distance of a derelict area, or where large sites are being stripped for building development in the vicinity, it is worth organizing the removal of the topsoil and using it for immediate coverage. Topsoiling one acre of land to a depth of nine inches requires 1,210 cubic yards of soil and the cost of digging and transporting this a few hundred yards can be greater than the average value of agricultural land in the locality. Therefore careful and fine judgment is often essential in determining the depth of topsoil to be laid.

As little as three inches of topsoil can suffice to provide a grass sward on good filling provided the topsoil spreading and grass sowing are done quickly before the soil has had time to erode away. Where agricultural processes and cultivations are proposed, the minimum depth should be twelve inches of good soil. Under really bad conditions of filling, as for instance where deleterious material, heavy clay, gault, ash or rock has to be covered, or where the topsoil itself is of poor quality, it may be necessary to provide two feet thickness or more of topsoil before satisfactory surface conditions can be obtained.

The British Standards Institution has recently produced a publication dealing with topsoil classification. The new standard, B.S. 3882, describes some of the more important qualities of various topsoils and classifies three characteristics, namely:

(a) Texture (light, medium and heavy).
(b) Lime content (ranging from acid to alkaline, with the related pH values).
(c) Stone content (ranging from stone-free to extremely stony).

These classifications can be used with advantage to describe the materials required in all specifications dealing with topsoil which is required for reclamation purposes.

After topsoiling, careful husbandry is essential for about five years during which there should be a steady improvement in the soil structure. This entails preparation of a programme of cultivation, fertilization and cropping, adapted to the nature of the soils on the site and to the weather conditions in the district. The land is generally ploughed and disced prior to sowing with grass, under which it may remain for four or five years before the second ploughing and reseeding. Where an arable rotation is adopted, the land may be cropped with wheat for two years and then sown down to a grass ley for a further two years. Such a ley will be made up of a mixture of Italian and perennial rye-grass together with red clover. By such husbandry the condition of the soil is built up and the amount of organic nitrogen in the soil is increased by the inclusion of red clover. Following the ley the land can again be cropped as required. During the whole of the period, lime with straight and/or compound fertilizers are applied as necessary, usually at about double the normal rate. At the onset, skeleton drainage only may have been installed

127

and the permanent system may then be completed in the fourth or fifth years, accompanied by mole ploughing and subsoiling. Where this work has to be carried out, it should be done in dry weather so as to break up the compaction of the soil and promote natural drainage. There can be no set treatment applicable to all sites—treatment should always be flexible and the conditions at each site should be reviewed at the end of each year, when the programme for the following year can be prepared to meet requirements. (See Plate 35.)

Agricultural Grants

Grants and financial assistance are available to farmers for improving the quality of land and for reclaiming waste or derelict land. It is essential that the land concerned should form part of a farm unit equipped with buildings, before the Ministry of Agriculture, Fisheries and Food can give assistance. Where this condition can be satisfied a grant may be payable under the Farm Improvement Scheme, at the rate of one-third of either the actual cost of the work or of the prescribed standard cost of certain specified items, such as claying and marling, fencing, etc. Precise details can be found in Statutory Instrument No. 627/1958—The Farm Improvements (Standard Costs) Regulations 1958.

The 'Assistance Grant for Small Farmers' is a scheme which provides for grants up to a limit of £1,000 for field husbandry—this may include the improvement and renovation of grass land and related reclamation work. Later on, ploughing grants of £5 per acre (currently at December 1964) may be available for tilling the land.

The Ministry of Agriculture also operates schemes whereby farmers can obtain financial assistance towards the costs of fertilizers and lime used on agricultural land. For example a grant of about £7 a ton is made for sulphate of ammonia and £4 16s. 0d. a ton (minimum quantity 4 cwt) in respect of superphosphate (December 1964). Refunds are also made towards the costs of liming land where the amount of lime used exceeds two tons. In this instance, the contribution, calculated on plot rates, cannot exceed 75 per cent of the farmer's gross cost of lime, transport and spreading. Details of the Fertilizers Scheme are available in Statutory Instrument No. 961/1964 and of the Lime Scheme in Statutory Instrument No. 903 of 1964.

Where works of drainage are carried out, the owners and occupiers of agricultural land may be entitled to grants towards the costs of field drainage. The grant generally amounts to about 50 per cent of the net cost of approved work. (See Plates 36 and 37.)

Pioneer Vegetation

After filling, grading and surface restoration, the next step is the establishment of pioneer vegetation, that is, vegetation which has low nutritional requirements and which by its root action and the deposition of litter and decayed organic matter raises the soil quality to approach normal fertility levels. Over a long period of time this restoration of condition occurs naturally and in this country the usual stages of succession for pioneer vegetation are—lichen and mosses; miscellaneous weeds and weed grasses; legumes; a scrub of thorn, gorse and bramble; then shrubs and small trees such as elder, birch and willow.

When agricultural land is neglected and has deteriorated, it generally goes back to the scrub stage but in the restoration of derelict industrial sites, it is usually necessary to go further back and to start at the grass and weed stage and then to grow a selected succession of plants of this type suited to the prevailing conditions. These plants, when growing, will set in motion and accelerate processes in the restoration of soil condition to a fertility level which becomes eventually acceptable for agricultural usage. Generally speaking, grasses and legumes are used either singly or in combination for sowing down restoration sites and when the initial seeding takes place it is important to ensure that the soil is well supplied with readily available plant nutrients to allow as good an establishment and growth of the young seeds as possible, from the outset. This will entail a proper assessment of the need to supply lime, phosphate, potash and nitrogen, not only for the early establishment phase, but also later on to ensure continued growth of the established sward. In this way, condition in the soil will be more rapidly built up and the restored site maintained in a vigorously growing state. In all this work, invaluable help and advice can be freely obtained from the regional and local officers of the National Agricultural Advisory Service of the Ministry of Agriculture, Fisheries and Food. These officers have a wide experience of regional conditions and problems and in addition they can call upon a vast reservoir of research and experimental information.

It is generally best to cultivate from seed those grasses and plants that are normally employed in agriculture and therefore most easily available. Certain perennial weeds and a few sedges and rushes are occasionally useful, especially under adverse conditions, but weeds must be carefully chosen in agricultural areas to avoid nuisance to farmers. Noxious weeds must be avoided; in particular, spear thistle, creeping or field thistle, curled dock, broad-leaved dock and ragwort are classified as pernicious weeds and the spreading of these in agricultural districts is illegal.

Grass Seed Mixtures

Of all pioneer vegetation, the grasses are unquestionably the most useful and ubiquitous. They are tolerant of a wide range of environment and they have highly developed root systems that extract the maximum nutrient from soil, enabling them to survive under conditions fatal to most other plants. On hill slopes the root systems can bind loose surfaces and prevent erosion and on all surfaces the grasses carpet and protect the soil with a fresh green herbage that lives and has scores of uses.

In the past, the practice was to sow a seed mixture containing many different species and strains in the hope that a proportion at least would succeed. But in recent years a great deal of work has been done at research stations and experimental grounds, particularly at Aberystwyth, where most valuable strains have been selected and bred for their specific qualities. These strains are generally known under the 'S' code numbers which have been assigned to them. Present-day policy is to use the strains alone or in mixtures containing only a few strains chosen as appropriate for the situation, soil and purpose for which they are sown.

For general purposes, perhaps the most widely used are Perennial Ryegrass (S.23), Cocksfoot (S.26), Timothy (S.48), and Italian Ryegrass (S.22). They often form the basis of mixtures with White and/or Red Clover and other herbage plants. For heavy clay soils, the bulk of the mixture might be Perennial Ryegrass with some Brown Top and a little White Clover. In the case of light soils, Perennial Ryegrass might be mixed with Cocksfoot and White Clover.

To ensure good germination, the seed mixtures should be sown at times when a period of moisture and warm sunshine can reasonably be expected, say from late March to early May during the Spring season and from late Summer to early Autumn.

SUITABLE GRASSES AND PLANTS

Where the reclaimed land is in reasonable condition and where topsoil has been spread, the following grasses and plants are most commonly used. Their characteristics and the favourable conditions for their use are briefly described.

Italian Ryegrass (*Lolium multiflorum*)　This is a biennial grass dying out in its second year but having the advantage of rapid establishment even under somewhat adverse conditions. It is ideal as a short-term 'pioneer' crop to begin the process of soil conditioning. It grows in erect tufts and does not spread.

Perennial Ryegrass (*Lolium perenne*)　As its name implies this is a long lasting grass of which many varieties of different growth habit are commercially available. Given reasonable conditions this grass will readily become established during the seeding year and provided it is adequately fertilized it will persist but it can lose its perennial nature to become a biennial. It prefers moist, fertile conditions but will grow on lighter soils when properly cared for. It constitutes the bulk of most grass seed mixtures but it is important to choose the variety linked to the circumstances under which it is grown. It is sometimes known as Red Darnel.

Cocksfoot (*Dactylis glomerata*)   This is a large coarse tufted perennial grass of which a number of varieties of different growth habit are commercially available. It becomes rapidly established from seed and grows over a wide range of soil conditions, doing better than perennial ryegrass where the soils are liable to dry out and are on the light side. Its maximum growth occurs in its second or third season and it can withstand drought provided the soil is sufficiently deep to allow its root system to develop. It produces a large amount of top and bottom growth and after cropping or mowing, it shoots up again rapidly and plentifully, producing a good aftermath. Care may be needed in the management of established sward to prevent it getting out of hand.

Red Fescue (*Festuca rubra*)   A number of forms and varieties of Red Fescue are available commercially, all of which are persistent and hard wearing. Care is required in preparation of the seed bed owing to the small size of the seed, but once established it forms a dense turf capable of surviving under poor conditions of soil fertility. The creeping Red Fescue is a widely-distributed perennial on both wet and dry soils and includes a number of varieties that spread extensively by underground rhizomes and withstand cold and drought. It develops in the second year after sowing and will grow at high altitudes making a good binding bottom grass which is useful on slopes.

Bent Grass (*Agrostis spp.*)   A number of forms of Bent are available, the more common being Brown Top (*A. tenuis*) and Creeping Bent (*A. stolonifera*). Seed of the former is readily available commercially to give a perennial low-growing type of grass. The seed is extremely small and needs ideal conditions for sowing. Creeping Bent has a creeping habit of growth and requires moist soil conditions. Seed is not usually available commercially but it is sometimes established vegetatively by planting out part of its creeping stolons.

Smooth Stalk Meadow Grass (*Poa pratensis*)   A low-growing, widely distributed perennial grass which spreads extensively by rhizomes and thrives in loose textured and light soils. Therefore it is suitable for sowing on banks and slopes to hold and bind the surface. It is the famous Kentucky Blue Grass of the United States. Being small seeded it requires good seed bed conditions for sowing and its development from seed is slow but when established the broad leaves spread to form a close matted and persistent turf which is not unduly affected by drought. It is not a suitable grass for heavy compact soils.

Red Clover (*Trifolium pratense*)   A number of forms of Red Clover are available commercially, and for soil restoration purposes they are generally used in mixtures with Italian and Perennial Ryegrasses for temporary leys of one or two years duration in an arable rotation. They are fairly rapidly established and are capable of building up nitrogen in the soil naturally.

White Clover (*Trifolium repens*)   A creeping perennial clover which is included in most long-term seed mixtures. This plant can grow where soil nitrogen is deficient and it is capable of taking nitrogen from the air into its root system thus enhancing soil conditions. It has been particularly useful in the rehabilitation of power station fly ash dumping sites.

Alsike Clover (*Trifolium hybridum*)   Has proved valuable on heavy soils for the provision of bottom growth.

Lucerne (*Medicago sativa*)   A deep-rooted perennial legume which has been extremely useful in restoration work particularly in ironstone workings. Owing to its deep and wide-ranging root system, it is one of the best soil structure improvers and consequently it is a most valuable pioneer crop. It thrives on a wide range of soils, particularly those containing a little lime, but it is extremely sensitive to soil acidity and the restoration area should be free draining to ensure establishment and good growth. It can withstand long periods of drought and it is largely used as a cutting plant rather than for grazing. It is also known as Alfalfa and Purple Medick.

PLANTS FOR THE MORE DIFFICULT SITES

Under the more difficult site conditions there are many other grasses and a wide variety of weeds and pioneer plants capable of being used successfully although they may not grow as quickly or as readily as the foregoing. The characteristics of a number that have already been used in various reclamation schemes are briefly described below. The choice of their use depends largely, of course, upon the site conditions and the effect which it is desired to produce.

Timothy Grass (*Phleum pratense*) A tufted perennial with shallow roots that tend to creep and spread. Very hardy and cold resistant, it succeeds best on moist heavy soils. Develops quickly from seed and is also well known as Cat's-Tail.

Yorkshire Fog (*Holcus lanatus*) A tufted hairy perennial which is a very common weed-grass growing on a wide range of soils under dry and wet conditions. Also known as Meadow Soft-Grass.

Rough Meadow-Grass (*Poa trivialis*) A widely distributed tufted perennial with shallow-rooted creeping stolons. Develops quickly on rich moist soils and stands up to atmospheric pollution. Also known as Rough Blue Grass.

Crested Dog's-Tail (*Cynosurus cristatus*) A small tufted perennial which is widely distributed and can withstand cold and drought. It is a 'bottom grass' which is useful for poor soils. Development is slow and little growth is produced in the seeding year. Slender foliage which stands up well to mowing.

Couch (*Agropyron repens*) A large tufted perennial which spreads extensively by creeping wiry rhizomes. A most tenacious weed which is difficult to eradicate but it can be useful in a soil-holding capacity on loose slopes and banks. It is commonly known as Twitch and each piece of rhizome is capable of developing into a fresh plant. Widely distributed.

Common Oat (*Avena fatua*) A number of oat-grasses develop quickly on poor soils.

Rye (*Secale cereale*)   Is useful for temporary seeding on poor soils.

Rape (*Brassica napus*)   Develops rapidly for grazing.

Field Beans (*Faba vulgaris*)   Are quick-growing plants especially on calcareous soils.

Lupins (*Lupinus polyphyllus*)   Are leguminous plants with an attractive flower spike. They are very suitable for poor sandy soils because they help to build up the fertility value by increasing the nitrogen content of the soil.

Ribwort (*Plantage lanceolata*)   This is a weed that provides useful bottom growth on almost every type of soil and it can withstand long periods of drought.

Yarrow (*Achillea millefolium*)   This is a useful weed for sowing on banks because its creeping rootstock spreads and binds the surface. It will grow in poor sandy soil and withstands drought quite well.

Furze or Gorse (*Ulex europaeus*)   A leguminous, thorny flowering shrub which develops slowly but gives good cover when established. It will grow in poor slightly acid soil and tolerate dry conditions. It reaches a height of six feet and has an attractive yellow flower.

Broom (*Cytisus scoparius*)   This is another leguminous flowering shrub. It develops quicker than gorse and will grow on poor soil and withstand drought.

Rest Harrow (*Ononis spinosa*)   A perennial low shrub of wide occurrence which is also known as Cammock. The rootstock is tough and has binding qualities because it spreads by rhizomes. The shrub is often spiny, has pink flowers and is leguminous.

Tufted Vetch (*Vicia cracca*) and **Bush Vetch** (*V. sepium*)   Leguminous perennials which thrive on a wide range of alkaline soils and are able to withstand drought. Attractive blue and purple flowers.

Rosebay Willow Herb (*Epilobium angustifolium*)   A handsome plant with purple flowers which grows to a height of five feet and seeds readily on waste land, chiefly on light soils and under moist conditions. It has a perennial creeping rootstock.

Charlock (*Sinapis arvensis*)   Also known as Wild Mustard, is an annual belonging to the cabbage family. It likes a light dry soil and it has bright yellow flowers.

Common Pearlwort (*Sagina procumbens*) This is a perennial that forms a low tuft with matted root growth. It produces small white flowers.

Lesser Celandine (*Ranunculus ficaria*) A plant with bright golden flowers and roots which produce a large number of tubers making it capable of rapid reproduction.

Cranesbill (*Geranium molle*) A pink-flowered annual with tough matted rootstock.

Red Poppy (*Papaver rhoeas*) An annual that seeds easily in freshly turned ground.

Haresfoot Trefoil (*Trifolium arvense*) A type of clover with pinky-white flowers, and which prefers dry, light soils.

Silverweed (*Potentilla anserina*) A yellow-flowered weed of wide occurrence which sends out runners from its rootstock and prefers moist conditions.

Bramble (*Rubus fruticosus*) A tough thorny plant with a perennial rootstock which grows vigorously and rapidly everywhere. It has pink and white flowers and its fruit is the edible blackberry.

Dog Rose (*Rosa canina*) This is the largest British wild rose and it has pink or white flowers. Of widespread occurrence, it forms a thorny bush of considerable size when established.

Coltsfoot (*Tussilago farfara*) This plant has a bright yellow flower and it seeds readily in stiff clay soil. It has a thick perennial rootstock with spreading offshoots and large radical leaves (i.e. leaves rising direct from the rootstock).

Catsear (*Hypochoeris radicata*) A perennial that has a tap root, radical leaves and a yellow flower; it prefers moist conditions.

Dandelion (*Taraxacum officinale*) A perennial of widespread occurrence which seeds easily. It has a golden yellow flower, radical leaves and a tough penetrating root.

Wild Chicory (*Cichorium intybus*) A perennial which flourishes under dry conditions, especially in chalk districts. It has bright pale blue flowers, radical leaves and a long, thick fleshy rootstock.

Heather or Ling (*Calluna vulgaris*) A plant of widespread occurrence which tolerates poor soils and dry conditions. It has small purple flowers and tough, wiry roots and stems.

Field Bindweed (*Convolvulus arvensis*)   A common weed with pink and white flowers. It is a perennial with extensive creeping rootstock and vigorous growth.

Motherwort (*Leonorus cardiaca*)   A hardy perennial which will flourish in poor soil. Grows to a height of four feet and has pink or nearly white flowers in a long terminal spike, which secrete a nectar that is particularly attractive to bees.

UNUSUAL TECHNIQUES

Within recent years considerable advances have been made in soil-conditioning techniques. It is now possible to treat problem soils with these conditioners so as to induce favourable seed germination and plant growth but the lower costs of the traditional methods of restoring soil fertility will ensure that they remain predominant as far into the future as can be foreseen, particularly where restoration is on a large scale and affects a wide area. However, a machine has been devised which will drill a mixture of seeds, fertilizers and polyelectrolyte resin soil conditioner. This conditioner is claimed to have the effect of aggregating problem soils into the optimum 'crumb-structure' favourable to plant growth and to be capable of maintaining this structure for years in spite of the disintegrating attacks of rain, frost, drought and soil bacteria. In conjunction with normal agricultural operations the conditioner has been shown to give increased germination and more rapid growth owing to a capillary uptake of water, increased aeration and greater availability of soil nutrients. Even at the extra costs, the use of this technique might be justified if it promotes vegetation where otherwise it would be impossible to establish the seeds as for example on the face of a steep slope.

The National Coal Board has experimented at Brodsworth in the West Riding and at Ollerton, Nottinghamshire, with planting out, as opposed to seeding by using sets of Creeping Bent

(*Agrostis stolonifera*) (Z.103) sometimes known as 'Emerald Velvet' lawn grass. The problem at these colliery spoilheaps was to reduce their harsh impact upon the landscape. Regrading and reshaping of the tips was physically impossible and access to the tips was very restricted. The sets of Creeping Bent were planted at one foot intervals on the steep slopes of the spoilheap and they quickly became established and spread giving a thin cover of vegetation with its more pleasing colour.

Where land has to be reclaimed for playing fields, sports grounds or similar uses requiring a large extent of turf, a satisfactory grass surface can be created by seeding, if suitable and good seed is used and provided it is protected during germination from birds and from high winds. For exceptionally fine lawns, such as bowling greens, it may be advisable to lay turf. There are several examples throughout the country of bowling greens having been created on the levelled waste and spoil of a former derelict site by the successful laying of sea-washed turf on a carefully-prepared base.

In cases where it has proved impossible to protect germinating seed from birds and high winds by normal precautions, the necessary protection from avian and aeolian ravages can be found in the following procedure. The surface soil should be thoroughly raked over for a depth of three or four inches and the selected seed should be evenly and thickly sown over the whole area. Immediately afterwards a thin layer of about one-eighth of an inch thickness of sharp sand should be spread and rolled with a heavy hand roller to give a firm surface. The surface is then lightly pressure-sprayed with a 55 per cent bitumen emulsion at the rate of one gallon to seven or eight square yards. As soon as the emulsion has broken, another eighth of an inch of sand is spread and rolled. By this method 90 per cent germination should occur within nine or ten days if the air temperature is continuously above 8 deg. Centigrade.

When playing fields and similar uses are provided on derelict land the final grading of the top layers of filling must be carefully done and this is as important as the final surfacing for the purposes of drainage. Very heavy mechanical equipment should not be used because this gives a too intensive compaction which holds water in the surface layer. The whole of the filling and surfacing should be pervious to a depth of at least two feet.

The possibilities of establishing allotments, smallholdings or market gardens on reclaimed land should not be ignored, particularly if supplies of good organic manures are available to raise the fertility levels. Several allotments have been successfully established on old pit heaps in mining districts and quite a number of smallholdings and market gardens have been developed on former gravel workings in most parts of the country. For smallholdings, Russian Comfrey (*Symphytum peregrinum*) has been suggested as a plant requiring deep, stiff soils and likely to thrive on derelict land in cold localities.

It is a perennial that can be cut five or six times between April and November, yielding up to sixty tons of cattle fodder per acre per year or it can be converted into ensilage of high protein content (24 per cent of the dry matter). However, because the roots must drive deeply, the plant is not suitable for thin soils over rock or peat or in districts where the water-table is close to the surface. The comfreys are stimulated by cutting and they are reputed to have no insect pests and to be almost immune to disease.

Hydraulic Seeding

Another technique known as 'hydraulic seeding' has been developed recently for sowing grass seed where there are the adverse conditions of poor soil and steep slopes. Originally devised for the rapid improvement in appearance of highway cuttings and embankments in North America the technique has now been improved and extended to cover all raw earth workings. The seed mixture and fertilizers are mixed with water and sprayed under pressure over the raw surface to be treated. This is then covered with a mulch of chopped straw and bitumen emulsion which is also spread by spraying over the surface. The two operations can be combined when wood cellulose fibre is used instead of chopped straw.

Soil analyses should be made before attempting hydraulic

seeding, because an analysis facilitates the choice of the most appropriate seed species to suit the location and site conditions as well as enabling the fertilizers to be designed to meet any nutrient deficiencies in the soil. The analysis will also reveal any toxic conditions and indicate the pH status. This information enables remedial treatment to be prescribed and to be applied, either before or during the sowing.

The mulch performs a number of important functions. It protects the seed from wind and birds during germination and the period of initial growth. It prevents erosion by reducing the rainfall run-off and increasing the absorption of water. It insulates the seed and young plant from temperature extremes, shielding it from frost and burning sun. It forms a nidus for micro-organisms and insect life, thus promoting, in an even and relatively warm temperature, a 'forcing' environment.

Although the sowing of grass is the most obvious and usual use of the technique, it can be applied to the sowing of almost any seed. It expedites the establishment of all types of pioneer vegetation and even shrubs and trees can be propagated by the process.

The operation of hydraulic seeding is economical and it can be carried out very rapidly over a large area. Where only a cosmetic treatment is required it usually makes topsoiling unnecessary and, under the worst conditions, it reduces the amount of topsoil required. Where a grazing use is required it is advisable to provide a layer of topsoil and where cultivations and agricultural uses are envisaged, topsoiling will remain essential.

Hydraulic seeding is very much cheaper than laying turf and the resulting sward is likely to be more free from weeds. The seed can be sown immediately on a graded surface comprising subsoil, as left by the earth-moving equipment and without any cultivation or the preparation of a seed-bed. The bituminous emulsion used for binding the mulch is relatively stable and is unlikely to break up until vegetation is firmly established. The technique can be operated all the year round in almost every part of the country and the plant used (see Plates 38 and 39), is mobile, so that few sites are inaccessible to it.

CHAPTER 9

Tree Planting

In all instances where derelict land cannot be reclaimed for a more economic use, the planting of trees should be undertaken for the purposes of timber production and landscaping. There are certain circumstances, too, in which tree planting should be undertaken even though the site could be reclaimed for a more profitable use. In barren or dismal surroundings the refreshment value of trees is most pronounced, notwithstanding the fact that this value cannot be expressed in financial terms. It is still contended that derelict sites in remote or rural areas can offend but few and therefore no money need be wasted upon them and they should remain without any remedial treatment. Advocates of this policy would let nature heal the scars however long it takes or however much the countryside is disfigured. Such an attitude cannot really be justified in a civilized community or reconciled with an affluent society.

Furthermore, Britain is very deficient in woodlands, plantations and trees compared with most other countries. It has 6·88 per cent of its area occupied by woodlands whereas the average for Europe is 29·8 per cent of the land surface covered by forest. In Finland the figure is as high as 71·8 per cent; Sweden has 56 per cent; U.S.S.R. has 50·7 per cent; Canada has 45·7 per cent; U.S.A. has 34·4 per cent; West Germany has 29·2 per cent; Norway and Switzerland have 24·4 per cent; France has 21·1 per cent and Italy has 19·7 per cent of its area under trees.

Planting Methods

There is no difficulty in obtaining satisfactory results in the afforestation of derelict land provided the soil has not been poisoned by industrial wastes, exposure is not too severe, atmospheric pollution is not excessive and that some protection is afforded against children and animals until the trees are well established. In the first year after planting there may be a loss of 10 per cent but even under unfavourable conditions the loss is unlikely to exceed 15 per cent and this is supportable. The total costs of preparation of a derelict site, planting, fencing, beating-up, thinning, and general supervision for the first five years (and that is the most expensive period) need not exceed £60 an acre on a sizeable holding.

In the past, when trees have been planted on derelict sites or spoilheaps in this country it has been the general practice to level the ground and excavate a large hole before planting each tree in a filling of good soil mixed with manure or peat, to retain moisture. But this elaborate procedure is by no means essential and excellent results have been obtained merely by mattock planting or with the minimum excavation, just sufficient to take the roots comfortably and without the importation of specially prepared soil. Levelling can give rise to adverse conditions for trees owing to soil compaction; many species appreciate the open consistency of various spoils and wastes. More use too, is being made now, of seedlings raised in fibre or cardboard pots; these seedlings are just planted in their containers which are allowed to rot away. Where atmospheric pollution is severe and on exposed sites it is essential to plant a large proportion of a nurse species which will give shelter from wind, provide shade, build up humus in the soil, stabilize the surface and help to retain moisture.

In planting derelict sites it is also important to have regard for those design features which will ensure retention of moisture at the roots. Perhaps we have something to learn of the value which terracing has in the retention of moisture (or to re-learn, if the evidence of our ancient lynchets is accepted). It is particularly evident when steep slopes have to be planted, that surface stability can be secured and gullying erosion can be averted if a shallow terracing is formed (either horizontally or spirally) with a pronounced slope into the hillside. Terracing is a particularly favourable form of treatment where planting has to be carried out on steep sides of pits, depressions and quarries. The terraces can be of a similar pattern and profile to those which have been evolved in hot countries. Remarkable plantations can be seen on the arid mountain slopes of Syria and Israel and even in Italy, where vineyards and olive groves have been formed on 'gradoni' and have become established under most adverse conditions. A striking example was the afforestation of the hills around the Lake of Galilee and above Tiberius where repeated failures had been experienced until terracing was adopted.

For the conventional forestry spacing, trees should be planted at five-foot intervals and thinned out when a good canopy has formed. However, wider spacing is nowadays acceptable for most reclamation planting and where the objective is a wood rather than an economic plantation it would be sensible to plant rather wider. Well balanced transplants or saplings which have been raised under hardy conditions should be chosen and the species that possess pioneer characteristics are preferable. That is, species having low nutrient demands, a vigorous and penetrating rootstock and the capacity for retaining moisture. Species which are deciduous, are particularly valuable because they provide litter and are thereby able to build up the organic content of the surface soil.

When local authorities have considerable areas of dereliction within their boundaries they should find it advantageous to establish a tree nursery in order to produce stock which is especially suited to reclamation work. Very often, such stock would comprise species which are not readily available commercially because they are not in popular demand, as for instance, rooted willow cuttings, grey alder or white poplar. These can be mass produced quite cheaply in a municipal nursery and by annual lifting and judicious root pruning, special stock can be produced which has a close, well developed, fibrous root-ball. A wider choice of species capable of vigorous growth is available in the warmer districts of the south and in the damp western districts than is generally available in the southern and eastern parts of the country.

Tree planting is always a long-term solution for visual problems but a tree cover sufficient to clothe all scars should be available within ten years of planting and it would be obviously young woodland in twenty years but it may be as long as forty years before the woodland becomes an established feature of the landscape. Plantations sit better in the landscape when they are not of regular shape and it is always desirable to avoid straight boundaries. Judicious mixtures of hardwoods, softwoods, deciduous and coniferous species are likely to yield the most pleasing results from a scenic standpoint, because such mixtures present endless seasonal variations and splendid contrasts in outlines, textures and shades of colour.

Forestry Grants

The Forestry Commission makes grants for three types of planting schemes which are differentiated as (i) The Dedicated Woodlands Scheme, (ii) The Approved Woodlands Scheme, and (iii) The Small Woodlands Scheme. These grants may be obtained for tree planting on derelict land, provided an economic crop of timber can be reasonably expected, but it must be acknowledged that not all derelict sites are suited to these grants and in some cases it might not be feasible to aim at economic standards. Free technical advice on the general suitability of any scheme is available from officers of the Forestry Commission on application to the appropriate Conservator of Forests.

(i) **Dedicated Woodlands** This scheme provides the most comprehensive form of assistance. The owner enters into a Covenant Agreement with the Forestry Commission, by which he undertakes to manage the woodlands for the main purpose of timber production in accordance with an agreed Plan of Operations and under skilled supervision. In return, financial assistance is provided in the form of a planting grant and an annual management grant. The planting grant is currently (at December 1964) £22 4s. 0d. per acre for every acre satisfactorily planted, replanted or otherwise restocked, after the date of dedication. Partial planting is treated *pro rata*. The annual maintenance grant is currently (December 1964) at the rates of £1 per acre for the first hundred acres, 13s. 6d. for the second hundred acres and 8s. 6d. per acre for the remainder.

Alternatively, an owner may elect, at the outset, to receive financial assistance under another arrangement, whereby he will receive 25 per cent of the approved net annual expenditure on the dedicated woodlands, until such time as they become self-supporting. If the owner adopts this basis, he must keep accounts in a prescribed form.

An owner in dedicating his woodlands, binds himself and his successors in title, not to use the dedicated land for any purpose other than forestry, but provision is made for a relaxation of this covenant should exceptional circumstances arise. If a dedicated woodland changes hands, the successor in title is invited to continue to manage it under the approved Plan of Operations, and if he undertakes to do so, he becomes entitled to the appropriate grants.

Management of the woods for timber production need not mean the exclusion of sport or disregard for amenity, but rather their reconciliation with the needs of good silviculture. A trained forester is normally employed to meet the requirement of skilled supervision. Forestry Commission officers inspect the woodlands at regular intervals and give technical advice.

Perhaps it should be noted here that the Durham County Council has entered into a dedication agreement with the Forestry Commission, in respect of some 200 acres, which included derelict woodland, waste land and colliery spoilheaps.

(ii) **Approved Woodlands** This scheme is a modification of the dedication covenant, inasmuch as it omits the long-term binding arrangement and the maintenance grants. The owner undertakes to manage the woodland in accordance with a Plan of Operations approved by the Forestry Commission and in return receives a planting grant similar to that under the dedication scheme. This grant is currently (December 1964) £22 4s. 0d. per acre and £16 13s. 0d. of this is paid in the year of planting. The balance of £5 11s. 0d. is paid five years later, provided the woodland has become established and has been properly maintained.

(iii) **Small Woodlands Scheme** This scheme provides financial assistance for the planting or replanting of small woods or pieces of ground suitable for tree planting where the owner does not wish to enter into a comprehensive plan of management. The scheme may embrace (*a*) detached blocks, and narrow strips and belts provided that they are at least three chains wide and less than five acres in extent, and (*b*) detached blocks of bad access, not exceeding fifteen acres if of good shape, but up to thirty acres if the shape is bad.

A minimum area of one acre in one block must be completed each year. The owner's primary intention must be the production of timber and the species planted must be a sound choice for the site for this purpose. The site must be such that there is every reason to believe that timber production of not less than fifty hoppus feet per acre per annum mean annual increment will be obtained.

The current rate of grant is £22 4s. 0d. (December 1964) per acre for schemes which must be approved before planting begins. The first instalment of £16 13s. 0d. per acre is paid in the year of planting and the balance of £5 11s. 0d. is payable when the plantation has become established and has been properly maintained for five years. No management grant is paid.

TREES SUITABLE FOR DERELICT LAND

A wide variety of trees have the pioneer qualities already outlined, but it is essential to review the circumstances at each site in order to be able to choose the species most likely to flourish.

Where conditions are severe the stock selected should be hardy, fast growing and able to withstand atmospheric pollution in addition to possessing the pioneer qualities. The characteristics of different species that have been used successfully in reclamation work and the conditions under which they may be most favourably employed are set out briefly below.

Alder (*Alnus glutinosa*)   An invaluable pioneer that builds up the nitrogen content of the soil and an excellent nurse species because it quickly provides shade and shelter. It prefers a damp situation but dislikes highly acid and peaty soils. Rarely exceeds forty feet in height and under poor conditions it may become merely a large bush. The Grey Alder (*A. incana*) will tolerate much drier sites and it has the useful property of spreading by root suckers.

Alder Buckthorn (*Rhamnus frangula*)   Also known as Black Dogwood, this tree is similar in appearance to the Alder. It is tolerant of a wide range of soils but prefers moist conditions.

Ash (*Fraxinus excelsior*)   A graceful tree that withstands smoke and exposed situations. It is tolerant of most soils but prefers a deep porous soil and moist conditions. Its roots extend deeply and it can attain a height of eighty to a hundred feet. Not an easy species to grow and generally only used for special landscaping reasons.

Beech (*Fagus sylvatica*)   A slow-growing tree which is hardy and wind firm but is unable to withstand atmospheric pollution. It grows naturally upon chalk, limestone or gravel soils and attains a height of a hundred feet. It produces a heavy crop of leaves which provide good shade and plentiful humus. The tree has a very handsome shape and it provides magnificent seasonal colourings.

Birch (*Betula pendula*)   This is the hardiest, most graceful and ubiquitous of the forest trees, penetrating farthest north and to the greatest altitudes. The shallow slender roots prefer a well-drained slightly acid soil. It withstands smoke conditions but in some instances it has been difficult to establish on unburnt shale tips. It can grow to a height of fifty to seventy feet.

Elder (*Sambucus nigra*) Cuttings take root very readily and the tree will grow to a height of twenty feet under moist conditions. No tree grows more rapidly in its early years and therefore it is most useful where a live screen or shelter has to be formed quickly.

Elm (*Ulmus*) A slow-growing tree of the lowlands and valleys which can attain a height of 120 feet. It requires fertile soil but is not fussy about texture. The three species most commonly met are the English Elm (*U. procera*), the Wych Elm (*U. glabra*) and the Smooth-leaved Elm (*U. carpinifolia*). All are susceptible to Dutch Elm disease and the Elm is used only for landscaping effect.

Gean or Wild Cherry (*Prunus avium*) This is a decorative tree that carries a heavy crop of white blossom in early spring. It is fairly fast growing and can attain a height of fifty feet. Thrives in most soils but prefers deep, well-drained, alkaline conditions. The Dwarf Cherry (*P. cerasus*) is sometimes planted on derelict sites as a bush.

Hawthorn (*Crataegus monogyna*) A very slow-growing tree whose height varies from a thick bushy growth of ten feet to a forty-foot tree. It is very hardy and will grow densely in exposed situations. Produces a heavy crop of berries and will often colonize widely. Growth is spiny and suitable for hedges, etc. Withstands temperature extremes.

Hazel (*Corylus avellana*) Grows almost anywhere but without good soil it remains a shrub from four to twelve feet in height. Well known for its 'lamb's tails' catkins and for its nuts or cobs. It is quick growing and useful as a nurse species, being quite common in the South and Midlands.

Holly (*Ilex aquifolium*) This is a slow growing but very hardy evergreen that withstands smoke, wind and coastal conditions. Usually a small tree but it can attain a height of forty feet. The leaves have spines and foliage is dense near the ground giving excellent shelter. It grows on a variety of soils and will accept shady conditions.

Hornbeam (*Carpinus betulus*) This tree is similar in appearance to beech but the trunk is ovoid and often fluted. It is especially tolerant of heavy clay soils and can attain a height of sixty feet but in poor soils it remains a small tree. It is windfast and will grow in shady conditions.

Laburnum (*Laburnum anagyroides*) A handsome small tree which is tolerant of most soils, growing easily under normal conditions to a height of twenty feet. It is leguminous and carries long racemes of golden flowers which cause it to be commonly called bean trefoil or golden chain.

Lime (*Tilia platyphyllos*) This is the large-leaved species which with the Common Lime (*T. vulgaris*) is in greatest use. It attains a height of eighty feet and is fairly tolerant of soil conditions but prefers deep moist rooting. It has attractive light green foliage and yellow flowers that produce an abundant nectar which is most attractive to bees.

Locust (*Robina pseudacacia*) A smoke resistant, hardy and fast-growing tree. Also known as False Acacia and White Laburnum, it is leguminous and grows to a height of seventy feet. It is suitable for poor or chalky soils but it is shallow rooting and should not be used in exposed situations.

London Plane (*Platanus acerifolia*) This tree, which attains a height of ninety feet is notable for its tolerance of atmospheric pollution. It has a straight trunk from which the outer layer of bark peels off each autumn and it grows well in most light soils but it has a preference for deep well-drained soils. It is not successful in the North.

Oak (*Quercus robur*) This the largest and longest-lived of our native trees. It is deep rooted and tolerant of most soils from deep sandy loam to clay. It attains a height of sixty to 120 feet and is very subject to insect attack and parasites but none are really troublesome. Its greatest disadvantage from the reclamation standpoint, is its slow rate of growth. The Holm Oak (*Q. ilex*) is evergreen but terribly slow growing and is only used for landscaping purposes. The American Oak (*Q. borealis*) is much faster growing than the native tree, tolerates poor sandy soils and colours well in autumn.

Poplars (*Populus*) These comprise the fastest-growing trees in Britain. Most of them are easily propagated by cuttings to make good planting stocks at two years. Poplars normally require moist fertile sites with a free root-run and they may be of more value for screening purposes than for planting on derelict sites. The Black Poplars, including the familiar Lombardy Poplar (*P. nigra italica*) are the best known, but for work on poorish sites the Balsam Poplars, especially *P. trichocarpa* and its hybrids, are likely to be of most value. The root growth of all Poplars is vigorous, widespread and penetrating and the tree withstands wind and exposure. Trees grow to a height of eighty to a hundred feet. White Poplar (*P. alba*) reaches a height of fifty feet and is excellent for checking erosion because it will grow in loose soil. The native Grey Poplar (*P. canenscens*) is tolerant of exposure and suckers freely. Care should be taken to plant varieties not susceptible to disease.

Rowan (*Sorbus aucuparia*) This attractive tree thrives almost everywhere and its hardiness and acceptance of any type of soil give it a wide range, extending to 2,500 feet above sea level. It grows naturally on slopes and hillsides and attains a height of thirty to fifty feet. It is also known as the Mountain Ash, Quickbeam and Witchen. Other plants will readily grow beneath it and it is often used as a nurse tree.

Sycamore (*Acer pseudoplatanus*) This is a tree that grows easily and rapidly to a height of sixty or seventy feet and thrives on a wide range of soils. It is strongly rooted and will accept exposed situations. Winged seeds ensure wide and easy reproduction. Occasionally it suffers from die-back.

Willows (*Salix*) Graceful and rapidly-growing trees for damp situations. The willows mostly used in reclamation work are the Sallow (*S. caprea*) the Grey Sallow (*S. cinerea*) and the Osier (*S. viminalis*). Some willows of dwarf habit are also used, such as the Creeping Willow (*S. repens*) and the Woolly Willow (*S. lanata*). Cuttings and offshoots of all types of willow grow readily but *S. daphnoides* is perhaps the fastest growing.

Conifers (*Pinaceae*) The conifers provide the softwoods of commerce. Most are highly susceptible to atmospheric pollution. The Scots Pine (*Pinus sylvestris*) will grow in poor stony soils and attain a height of a hundred feet at a moderate rate of growth. It develops a deep tap root and is wind firm. The lower branches die away giving the tree its characteristic appearance of a tall bare pole surmounted by a bushy top. Small trees under two feet in height are best for planting.

Lodgepole Pine (*Pinus contorta douglas*) is an excellent pioneer which has a fast rate of growth. The coastal strains will withstand severe exposure, high rainfall and infertile peaty soils, such as occur in the north and west of the country. The Black Pines (*P. nigra*) include the Austrian Pine (var. *austriaca*) which is perhaps the most resistant conifer to atmospheric pollution and the Corsican Pine (*P. nigra* var. *calabrica*) which grows to a height of 120 feet. Both will thrive in almost pure sand, fixing the sand dunes and providing shelter. They will withstand winds and are useful near the sea. Corsican Pine grows rapidly in lowlands under warm conditions and low rainfall.

The Beach Pine (*P. contorta*) is a smaller tree that grows well in light stony soils free from chalk and it gives good shelter in exposed places. The Mountain Pine (*P. mugo*) is a very hardy slow-growing tree, some forms of which are little more than bushes. It thrives on the poorer soils, will transplant very well and is suitable for planting on banks and slopes.

European Larch (*Larix decidua*) is a tree of the mountains, ascending to 7,000 feet above sea level where it will withstand prolonged cold conditions. It attains a height of 120 feet and has a very straight tapering trunk. The larch family is deciduous and in this respect differs from most conifers. They are generally good pioneers of raw subsoil material provided these are not too heavy and compact. The Japanese Larch (*L. leptolepis*) tolerates a wider range of conditions than the European species including greater exposure and less soil fertility. It grows very vigorously in early life and thrives on hillsides in high rainfall districts. Young trees under three feet in height are best for transplanting. Hybrid Larch (*L. eurolepis*) is a natural hybrid between European and Japanese larches which excels both, being hardier, more tolerant of difficult soil conditions and faster growing.

Norway Spruce (*Picea abies*) grows well on moist soils but not in acid or peaty locations or in exposed situations. Not suitable for those southern and eastern parts of the country where rainfall is less than thirty inches a year. Sitka Spruce (*P. sitchensis*) is a fast- and tall-growing tree of pyramidal habit which withstands exposure at high elevations and near the coast. It has a surface root system that thrives in wet, cold soil but dislikes long warm, dry periods. The Serbian Spruce (*P. omorika*) is a hardy evergreen which withstands atmospheric pollution better than most conifers and is best transplanted when under three feet in height.

Douglas Fir (*Pseudotsuga taxifolia*) is a quick-growing tree with a long straight trunk and pyramidal habit, which makes it suitable for screening purposes. It thrives on fertile slopes but is susceptible to windthrow. Adaptable to various soils except lime soils. Under humid and well-drained conditions it produces a dense shade which suppresses undergrowth.

Western Hemlock (*Tsuga heterophylla*) is easy to establish, quick growing and tolerant of poor soil conditions. Often used in mixture with Sitka Spruce.

In general, however, the spruces and firs are likely to be the lesser used of the conifers in reclamation work.

Plate 34. Derelict land reclaimed to provide sites for new industries at Tonypandy, Glamorganshire

Plate 35. Former gravel pits at Water Orton, Warwickshire, filled with pulverized fuel ash from Hams Hall electricity

Plates 36 *and* 37. Derelict land restored to agriculture at Coton Farm, Nether Whitacre, Warwickshire. (*above*) Filling operations in progress. (*below*) First barley crop being harvested

Plate 39. Hydraulic seeding—applying the mulch of chopped straw and bituminous emulsion

Plate 38. Hydraulic Seeding—spraying on seed mixture and fertilizers

Plate 40. Wilmington, Co. Durham, dominated by colliery spoilheap

Plate 41. Colliery spoilheap at Croxdale near Durham before planting in 1956. Note River Wear at base of spoilheap and mainline railway viaduct on left

Plate 42. Croxdale spoilheap in 1965 with trees well established. Mainline viaduct as reference point

CHAPTER 10

Landscaping and Amenity Treatment
(1) Spoilheaps

'The tip itself towered to the sky and its vast dark bulk, steaming, and smoking in various levels, blotted out all the landscape at the back of the village. Its lowest slope was only a few yards from the miserable clutter of houses. One seemed to be looking at a Gibraltar made of coal dust and slag.' Thus J. B. Priestley described one of these stark and sombre symbols of the coalfield. George Orwell had similar thoughts—'a slag-heap is at best a hideous thing because it is so planless and functionless. It is something just dumped on earth like the emptying of a giant's dustbin. On the outskirts of the mining towns there are frightful landscapes where your horizon is ringed completely round by jagged grey mountains and underfoot is mud and ashes and overhead the steel cables where tubs of dirt travel slowly across miles of country. Often the slag-heaps are on fire and at night you can see the red rivulets of fire winding this way and that and also the slow-moving blue flames of sulphur which always seem on the point of expiring and always spring out again.'

How bitter, sensitive people can become when they have to live in the shadow of such monsters. How they resent the general indifference with which spoilheaps are regarded by most people who live far removed from unsightly features. How they pour scorn on neighbours whose aesthetic perceptions have become blunted by their surroundings. It shocks the stranger to talk with persons whose feelings are so affected by their environ-

153

ment and who see the whole image of the coalfield in the heap which oppresses them.

Most spoilheaps whether they are of the high conical shape or long blackened escarpments or distorted fan ridges have been built regardless of any consideration beyond that of amassing as much spoil as possible upon a minimum tipping area. This gives them their unnaturally steep slopes, their monstrous bulk and height, their crude harsh outlines which must be discordant and out-of-scale in any humanized landscape. They are the very symbols of the coalfields contributing greatly to the general air of drab barrenness. In the absence of any remedial measures they must continue so, because the acute steepness of the slopes fosters erosion, gullying and sterile surfaces. When a number of spoilheaps are grouped together they give the impression of a lunar landscape and when they are combined with marlholes and other forms of dereliction they give the impression of a 'blitzed' area of massive devastation. (See Plate 40).

Configuration

The configuration of a spoilheap depends upon the type of equipment used in building it and upon the sequence of the tipping; both of these factors have their influence upon the techniques of landscaping. The shape, aspect and height of a spoilheap largely determine the intensity of exposure, the moisture content of the surface layers and consequently the degree to which vegetation can be promoted. Exposure is greatest on the upper slopes of high conical tips and least in the low sheltered hollows and re-entrants of fanned ridge tips which also retain moisture thus giving pioneer vegetation an opportunity to seed and establish itself. The conical tip generally remains grey and sterile but the sheltered pockets and troughs of the fan-ridge tip form seed-beds for weeds and grasses so that after a short time colonization starts moving slowly outwards to creep over the rest of the tip face, wherever it is not too steep for a hold to be established. All steeply sloping surfaces also suffer from gully erosion and a great deal of surface movement of extremely small particles. When spoilheaps remain quite sterile or are only very slowly colonized, it is generally due to the exposed surface conditions and to this continuous shifting of fine surface particles, which dry out in the high temperatures of the top layers and roll down the slope.

The natural, strongest and ultimate form of earth slopes is a concave curve with the flattest portion at the bottom. This form does not occur in man-made spoilheaps built by point-tipping equipment. Straight or convex slopes are almost invariably created and then slipping occurs and generally continues until eventually equilibrium is reached or some degree of approximation to the natural form is obtained. This happens more quickly with loose materials than with the heavier clays and shales or with materials that have some slight cementation property. Consequently the angles of repose can vary widely. In general they run from 14 degrees in the case of soft, wet earth, clays and peats, up to 48 degrees in the case of stiff clays, shales and stony wastes. Expressed as a ratio of base of slope to height this is a variation of from four to one (14 degrees) to a steepness of more than one to one (0·9 to 1 degree). A reasonably stable and natural angle of respose for almost every type of soil is 18 degrees that is, a ratio of three (base of slope) to one (height of slope).

Environmental Peculiarities

There are, of course, many other factors which can affect the growth of vegetation on spoilheaps and it is rare for the factors which prevail in one tip to be repeated exactly in the next. The chemical and physical properties of the soil in the tip are always important but the atmospheric and microclimatic conditions can be even more decisive.

The chemical composition of shales from the different coal measures varies, particularly in the amount of pyrites and sulphates which are contained. The reaction of newly-tipped shales is usually alkaline or basic but on weathering it becomes acid owing to oxidization of the sulphur compounds under moist conditions. Sulphuric acid is produced in the complex reduction of pyrites to ferrous sulphate thence to ferric sulphate and finally hydrolysis to ferric hydroxide (which gives the rusty colouration to water draining from tips). Spoilheaps which have a low pyrites content will generally remain neutral or alkaline in spite of weathering. The acid nature of a spoilheap can be toxic to vegetation for years and during this period it will seriously interfere with seed germination. Trees and shrubs are hardier and after weathering for a year or so, the acid nature of a tip should not normally preclude the growth of hardy species except possibly in small patches of high toxicity.

To support vegetation, a spoilheap must contain an adequate and easily available supply of nutrients and moisture and it must provide a stable surface in which roots can become established. The shales eventually weather to clay loams and they generally contain all the main nutrients in sufficient quantity and in an assimilable form. The amount of moisture can vary to both extremes in the same tip and it frequently does. There can be very wet conditions around the base of the tip and waterlogging can be seen in pockets and hollows higher up, while on the uppermost slopes there can be high surface temperatures and arid conditions. It should be noted also that spoilheaps often appear to have a perched water-table which may be due to capillary attraction and is analogous to the similar phenomenon in sand-dunes. The stability of the surface for rooting depends a great deal on the degree of exposure and upon the fineness of the surface soil particles. The degree or intensity of exposure depends in turn upon the amount of wind in the locality and the height of the surface relative to the surrounding district. Where the intensity of exposure is high it causes the surface layers to dry out rapidly and this is followed by erosion. When these surface layers consist of very small particles, such as the fine silt of washery wastes, they are continually moving and under these conditions germination can only occur extremely slowly, if at all.

Spoilheaps are found within industrial areas and in localities which have heavy atmospheric pollution. Smoke, fumes, soot and tarry deposits are inimical to vegetation and can be quite fatal when added to all the other adverse factors. However, the

Clean Air legislation is having a marked beneficial effect in industrial areas and with a careful selection of species and good design it is possible to achieve remarkable landscaping improvements with the spoilheaps. (See Plates 41 and 42.)

Regrading

In applying amenity treatment to spoilheaps and in designing landscape improvements the first problem is to introduce scale and reduce the artificial shapes to a more natural outline. Then there must be an effort to overcome their drab colouration and depressing appearance by clothing them with some form of vegetation—something living which reflects the changing seasons.

Where practicable the slopes should be regraded to inclinations not exceeding one in three, which besides giving them softer and more natural outlines, also reduces the tendency to erosion and gullying thus enabling vegetation to become established more quickly. At this gradient, too, it becomes much easier to manœuvre and operate earth-moving equipment which extends the scope for ground modelling and widens the landscaping possibilities.

The top of the tip should be formed into a dished plateau. All peaks and ridges should be levelled and graded with a final fall towards the centre of the plateau. This helps to reduce the amount of run-off and surface water drainage, with a consequent diminution of erosion and gullying. Spoil should be pushed into valleys and pockets to achieve a uniform grading and outline. In most cases regrading will result in an extension of the base of the tip and the coverage of a greater area.

Grassing

In many schemes, on completion of the regrading, a layer of topsoil has been provided to cover the shale, then lime and fertilizers have been applied and finally grass seed has been sown. The fundamental precautions to be observed are—very heavy liming (about two tons per acre) to neutralize the acid in the shale, heavy applications of fertilizers (approximately four hundredweights per acre) and a suitably selected seed mixture sown thickly at the rate of two hundredweights per acre. This has been accomplished at a cost of approximately £50 an acre. A thin green carpet can be expected within a few months of sowing, sufficient at least to put an end to dust and smell nuisance and to give a more pleasantly coloured aspect.

This method of treatment has been particularly successful in and near built-up areas and in localities where young tree plantations have been destroyed by vandalism. A number of local authorities have expressed a preference for grassing mounds and spoilheaps instead of planting them with trees because (*a*) Its beneficial effect can be seen and appreciated within six months whereas the results of planting are not apparent for many years. (*b*) The cost of protective fencing is avoided. (*c*) Grass is much less liable to be damaged by children, adults, stock and vermin, than is a plantation and (*d*) The possibility of failure through drought is more remote. Furthermore, the amenity treatment started with grasses and weeds can, of course, be carried further at any time by the planting of shrubs and trees.

Frequently, landscaping may be most successful where in essence it merely prescribes an acceleration of the natural processes, using heavy mechanical equipment to rapidly achieve natural angles of repose and choosing plant successions—grass, weeds, shrubs and trees—that hasten a cover of vegetation, thus achieving in a few years or even months, results which otherwise might take a century or more to reach.

Terracing and Planting

There are numerous examples of low spoilheaps that have been successfully planted with trees without any regrading and there are other instances where only partial regrading has been carried out before planting. (See Plate 43.) This is feasible where there are no steep and difficult slopes and where there are no great irregularities in profile. There are occasions too when general regrading and ground modelling are not practicable, as for instance, when the spoilheaps are very high, steep-sided and perhaps conical in shape. In these most difficult cases there is sometimes an opportunity for terracing treatment to mitigate the harsh impact of such discordant features.

The design of the terracing can vary enormously. In some circumstances only shallow terracing, a foot or so wide, may be possible—just sufficient to provide planting space. Normally terraces should be formed horizontally at vertical intervals of thirty to forty feet or they may be spiralled at a similar vertical interval. Where on the largest spoilheaps, angledozers can be used for sidelong cuts, a broad terrace should be formed twelve to fifteen feet wide. All terracing should be formed with a cross-fall from the outer edge into the tip. Trees should be planted nearer to the inner edge of the terrace and shrubs towards the outer edge. Tree planting should commence at the bottom of the spoilheap and very often only the bottom half of the tip need be planted to obtain a satisfactory visual effect. In any case planting should be stopped forty to sixty feet below the plateau which should form the top of the mound. The more extensive this plateau is, the better can the spoilheap eventually function as a place of public resort with viewpoints, picnic spots, etc. Access paths or rides should be arranged when tree thinning operations commence.

Wherever space is available and especially in rural areas, a shelter belt or plantation of trees and shrubs should be provided around the base of the spoilheap because this softens the junction line of the tip with its surroundings. As moist conditions prevail at the base of a tip, these plantations generally become quickly established and they then provide a windbreak for other planting on the higher slopes, reduce evaporation from the soil and afford some protection against cold air and frosts.

In the initial planting of all tips it is advisable to use a considerable proportion of alder, not only for its pioneer characteristics but also because it is so useful as a nurse species where exposure is severe or smoky atmospheric conditions prevail. Birch is also a sturdy pioneer, which can be widely used on burnt and unburnt spoilheaps. Poplars are most useful around the base and hawthorn, being tough, is frequently suitable for the intermediate slopes. After the pioneer species have become established other species and suitable forest trees can be planted. These should be of bushy and sturdy stock, not too large and certainly not lanky trees which are much more susceptible to wind damage. At the onset, trees on the upper slopes may be poor and stunted but they should improve as the plantation develops from the lower slopes upwards. Soil erosion will cease as soon as a canopy has been established but maintenance work may be necessary, to remedy occasional gullying and patches of slope erosion, by the use of dams, faggots, fascines, wickerwork revetting and staking.

A Pilot Survey

Some little time ago, the writer was asked to choose twelve colliery spoilheaps distributed over the country and to prepare a report on their amenity treatment. The terms of reference required them to be selected from major coalfields and to be (i) already in use on 1st July 1948 and being extended under cover of Class XX(3) of the General Development Order 1950 and (ii) eyesores which could be improved in appearance by regrading and planting. Estimates of cost were to be provided.

A preliminary examination was made of fifty-four spoilheaps within the coalfields of Nottinghamshire, Cannock, North Staffordshire, Warwickshire, Lancashire, Yorkshire, Glamorganshire and Monmouthshire. Twelve were then chosen and given detailed consideration. Estimates were prepared based upon a minimum schedule of the work necessary in each case at prices generally prevailing under normal contracting conditions. No provision for fencing was necessary because the spoilheaps were still in use and it would be impracticable to fence off portions of them. Owing to the atmospheric pollution prevailing at each site and in order to minimize trespass and vandalism, conifers were avoided and provision was made for planting the less attractive and cheapest pioneer trees such as alder, sycamore and thorn, to provide the initial amenity cover. The form of the spoilheaps and their surroundings with the suggested treatment and estimated costs are very briefly described below:

No. 1   A hogsback tip with conical peaks, in rural surroundings, covering some 24 acres and 130 feet high with slopes varying from 20° to 50°. The amenity treatment suggested included grading, planting with alder, sycamore, birch, thorn, gorse and broom. Estimated cost of engineering works £1,350. Planting £850. Total £2,200.

No. 2   Hogsback mounds covering 15 acres and 60 feet high with slopes of 30° to 50°. Directly opposite a large residential area and dominating a trunk road. Larger mounds were being formed behind and a useful screening effect could be produced in the amenity treatment which included regrading and planting with alder, sycamore, birch and poplar. Engineering works £2,000. Planting £900. Total £2,900.

No. 3   Flat-topped rectangular mound in semi-rural area covering 29 acres. Height varies from 60 feet to 90 feet and sides slope at 45°. North face dominates main road on outskirts of town. Treatment—regrading and planting with alder, sycamore, birch, thorn, broom, fescue and yarrow. Engineering work £1,300. Planting £900. Total £2,200.

No. 4   Three tips, a long shoulder and two conical peaks covering 21 acres. Height rises to 150 feet and slopes vary from 30° to 45°. Eyesore from main road and a place of popular public resort. Amenity treatment, grading, terracing and planting with alder, poplar, sycamore, birch and thorn. Engineering costs, £2,700. Planting £1,000. Total £3,700.

No. 5   Conical tip covering 8 acres and rising to a height of over 300 feet with a 40° slope. Mechanical tipping gear. An eyesore in a densely built-up area. Treatment— removal of apex, terracing and planting alder, sycamore, birch, poplars, broom and lupins. Engineering £2,600. Planting £700. Total £3,300.

No. 6 Fan-shaped tip spreading over 21 acres at varying levels up to 120 feet. Slopes from 25° to 40°. Treatment —regrading, terracing, planting with alder, sycamore, broom, yarrow and lupins. Engineering £2,460. Planting £1,120. Total £3,580.

No. 7 Irregular shape covering 45 acres, flat top, slopes vary from 20° to 45°. Tipping is by lorries and rail wagons. Regrading and planting with birch, sycamore, poplar, thorn, ash and grass sowing. Engineering £2,450. Planting £1,820. Total £4,270.

No. 8 Very conspicuous parallel hogsback tips with flat top being extended upwards. Over 30 acres and slopes 40° to 45°. Overhead gantry. Regrading, terracing, planting with alder, sycamore, birch, broom and lupins. Engineering £2,050. Planting £1,400. Total £3,450.

No. 9 Two active spoilheaps divided by a road and covering 17 acres with extensions over a further 23 acres. About 45 feet high, flat tops being extended upwards. Slopes vary from 30° to 40°. Grading and planting of alder, sycamore, birch and broom. Engineering £1,300. Planting £1,200. Total £2,500.

No. 10 Conical tip built by MacLane gear on the top of a hill covers 17 acres and is 250 feet to 300 feet high. Dominates town, valley, main road and is reputed to be visible 50 miles away. Treatment—removing top and grading; planting birch, ash, thorn, scrub oak and broom. Engineering £1,700. Planting £1,260. Total £2,960.

No. 11 Tipping has taken place at eight levels ascending the mountainside and extending to twin conical tips covering 15 acres on the crest. MacLane gear and tramway. Dominates a large built-up area. Treatment—grading and planting sycamore, birch, rowan, thorn and broom. Engineering £1,700. Planting £1,400. Total £3,100.

No. 12 Five tips ascending mountainside, four with plateaux and one conical. Dominates town and place of public resort. Treatment—removal of conical top, regrading and planting with alder, sycamore, birch, thorn, broom, yarrow and lupins. Engineering £2,700. Planting £1,260. Total £3,960.

The twelve spoilheaps served 15 colleries employing 18,500 men. The average cost of dealing with the spoilheaps was £3,176 per tip or £133 per acre.

Planting in Durham

The Durham County Council has perhaps planted more spoilheaps than any other local planning authority. The trees have been planted at five-foot centres, direct into the raw shale without the addition of soil or fertilizer. A mixture of conifers and hardwoods usually in the proportion of sixty to forty has been used. The conifers were generally three-year stock and the hardwoods were transplants twelve to twenty-four inches high. Soil analyses were made before planting and all reactions were acid with pH values varying between three and five. Acidity does not seem to have had any great effect on the growth. Of the conifers, Corsican pine and Lodgepole pine have been most successful and of the hardwoods, birch and grey alder have been the best and quickest growers. Costs of the work have varied between £45 and £52 an acre depending upon the amount of fencing and weeding done. Offset against these costs there has been a Forestry Commission grant of £21 an acre under a Dedication Scheme. The County Council is satisfied that the afforestation of pit heaps which has already been carried out has, in most cases, proved to be a practical and not too expensive method of improving the appearance of the countryside.

Regrading and Grassing in the West Riding

The West Riding County Council, on the other hand, has concentrated upon the regrading and grassing of spoilheaps and in this connection has recently devised a means of dealing with large tips which are still in use and where no form of planning control is available by reason of the General Development Order exemption. An agreement has been reached with the National Coal Board under the provisions of Section 37 of the Town and Country Planning Act 1962 whereby the county council undertook (at its own expense) a fairly substantial earth-moving job on the Bullcroft Colliery tip near Doncaster while the National Coal Board on their part undertook to restrict the height and general contours of future tipping on the heap. The spoilheap is clearly visible from the northern end of the Doncaster bypass road and it provided an unfortunate introduction to Yorkshire for motorists using A1 and approaching from the south. The end of the tip facing the Great North Road has been re-shaped so as to form a bank screening all future tipping activities from the vital viewpoints. After the spoil was re-positioned the screen bank was seeded down with a grass and clover mixture.

This idea of forming a screening bank has also been incorporated into planning consents for tipping within the West Riding. In the past it has been the custom to commence tipping close to the colliery and then expand outwards, thus always presenting an active tipping face to the public view. The West Riding has reversed this procedure and required tipping to commence in the form of a ridge along the boundary of the site farthest from the colliery so that the active tipping face is presented to the colliery whilst the face visible to the public is completed almost immediately and then graded and grassed. The screen bank so formed conceals all subsequent unsightly tipping and it has the advantage for the National Coal Board of quickly taking overburden and topsoil.

Lancashire

Lancashire has carried out both planting and seeding. In the early 1950s two trial reclamation schemes were successfully completed. The first project was the planting of a 10-acre colliery spoilheap at Bickerstaffe near Ormskirk and this led to the establishment of the county's own tree nursery and the preparation of a continuous planting programme. For the second project, a spoil heap at Bickershaw near Wigan was graded and experimental plots were set out and grass seeded. These trial schemes were followed by provision of a 15-acre sports field at Skelmersdale; the reclamation of 38 acres at Whalleys Basin for housing purposes and a sports stadium; the reclamation of 24 acres at Ince-in-Makerfield for housing and playing fields; regrading and restoration to agricultural use of 30 acres at Pennington Green and 180 acres south of Wigan. A further programme for the planting of 600 acres and the grading and reclamation of some 400 acres is now in hand.

The highly industrialized districts of Lancashire have made immense contributions to the national prosperity and the resultant dereliction is so extensive as to constitute one of the major planning problems in the county. A policy of reclamation has now been established and in many districts, the improvement in the environment is already quite spectacular.

CHAPTER 11

Landscaping and Amenity Treatment
(2) Flooded Excavations

The winning of minerals below the water table generally results eventually in an abandoned excavation which is flooded to a depth of from six to thirty feet, or even more in the case of flooded marlholes and quarries. Nearly half of the sand and gravel pits in the country are wet pits and the workings may be anything from twenty to 100 acres in extent. It has been estimated that some 22 million cubic yards of filling material would be required annually to keep pace with the current extraction of sand and gravel from wet pits. This amount of filling is just not available and even if it was, it would not be a good thing to fill up the wet pits because by partial filling and judicious planting (see Plates 44 a&b and 45) they can be converted into pleasant tree and shrub fringed lakes that vastly increase the amenity of the countryside. Probably about 500 acres of wet workings are worked out and abandoned by operators each year and as time goes on the number of unfilled wet pits is bound to increase, but with careful design in accordance with conditions attached to planning consents they can be transformed into greatly appreciated swimming, fishing, boating and water sports recreational areas.

A good illustration of what can be accomplished by the enterprise of a local authority is the 260-acre Midlands water sports centre at Chasewater (see Plate 46) near the edge of Cannock Chase. The Brownhills Urban District Council has created this popular amenity feature from derelict land affected by mining subsidence and an abandoned reservoir. The Council acquired the area and then provided roads, foreshore 'hards', a restaurant, car parks, club houses, an amusement park and a recreation camp. They also constructed a paddling pool, laid out gardens and planted trees and shrubs. The lake is about a mile long, half a mile wide and has about five miles of foreshore. Chasewater as it is now called, is used by sailing, hydroplane, speedboat, fishing and underwater exploration clubs as well as being an increasingly popular resort for the general public. At comparatively little cost, an excellent regional water sports centre has been provided from an unsightly derelict area and become a source of revenue, pleasure and recreation. Situated as it is on the periphery of the West Midlands conurbation and almost on Cannock Chase, this water sports centre must be of inestimable value as another outlet to cater for leisure pursuits in the shorter working week and its provision should increasingly reflect the wisdom of its sponsors.

Conversion Works

A survey of the flooded workings should be made and soundings should be taken so that accurate plans and sections can be prepared. From these the conversion works can be designed and costs can be estimated. The design will first have regard for safety and will then take into account the precise uses proposed after conversion and lastly there must be adjustment and sometimes reconciliation with the surroundings, whether they be urban or rural.

Very deep excavations, such as marlholes and quarries and occasionally sand and gravel pits are often partially filled so that over as large an area as possible the depth of water does not exceed eight feet. At the edges, shallow areas can be formed either by bulldozing high parts of the bank into the water or by cutting into the bank. An ample foreshore should be available around the lake and parts of it should be paved with stones or pebbles to form a foreshore 'hard' particularly at various points of access and where any craft are to be launched. Other parts of the foreshore should be levelled and planted with shrubs and trees. Much of the detailed design will depend on the uses proposed after conversion of the flooded excavation to an amenity water. Fishing, sailing, hydroplaning, water-skiing, speedboats and underwater exploration all demand different design features but all can be accommodated in one type of excavation or another and frequently a number of sports can be accommodated on the same lake when it is a large one. (See Plate 47.)

Promoting Fertility

When mineral workings cease and deep pits are abandoned they are frequently sterile and the waters are likely to be slightly acid. They may support no form of vegetable or other life and it may take a long period before even pioneer vegetation flourishes and fish appear and increase. In the shallow pits, as soon as the suspended matter settles, sunlight will penetrate to the floor of the pit and promote weed growth. At the same time vegetation becomes established around the margins of the pit and insects breed. It normally takes about three years before there is suffi- cient vegetable and animal life to support a few coarse fish and possibly eight to ten years before the water can be used as a fishery. By special treatment and stocking with aquatic plants, snails, shrimps and fish, the derelict workings can be brought into use and converted into fishing stretches more quickly—in perhaps three to five years. Angling clubs are expanding all over the country and the demand for fishing facilities is strong and growing. Therefore all efforts to increase fertility and hasten the conversion of abandoned workings are well repaid and most angling associations and organizations are prepared to assist in this work. Furthermore, there seems to be no reason why some of the smaller old workings could not be exploited as suppliers of fish food by entrepreneurs on a commercial scale.

For the development of fish life, alkaline waters are desirable and the pH value of the pit water should be ascertained. Waters of pH7 (neutral) or pH8 will need no treatment but lower pH values denote acidity and this should be counteracted by lime treatment. The normal method is to throw the lime (calcium carbonate) into the water from a boat so that the dosage is pretty even over the whole water. Waters of abnormal acidity may require as much as thirty to fifty hundredweights per acre, but the amount increases rapidly as the pH value falls. A dosage of 7 hundredweights per acre evenly distributed will suffice for a pH value of 6·5 and a further hundredweight will be required for a pH value of 6. If the pH value falls to 5·5 the dosage should be increased to 15 hundredweights per acre and for a pH value of 5 it will be necessary to deposit 24 hundredweights per acre. After giving the appropriate dosage, periodical tests should be made to ensure that the desirable alkalinity is maintained.

Fertilizers should then be applied, again from a boat, and they can be in the form of ordinary animal manures or chemical fertilizers, but they should be tipped and spread in the shallow waters around the margins of the lake. For the deeper waters (up to about eight to ten feet) liquid manure or chemical fertilizers should be poured or spread. The initial charge is usually sufficient to establish the organic cycle. Once plant life is established, the natural decay will maintain the supply of organic matter and promote the development of phytoplanton and floating plants without any further applications of fertilizers.

AQUATIC PLANTS

The common aquatic plants grow readily and after application of fertilizers many species are likely to appear spontaneously. However, better and quicker results can be obtained by deliberate transplanting and plants most suitable for the type of use proposed for the water can be chosen. It is perhaps more important to avoid weeds which might infest a water and if suitable plants become firmly established the objectionable types are often discouraged. The plant life of all lakes, ponds, canals and fishing waters in the surrounding countryside should be examined or if a local botanist can be consulted, this is the best course. Fishing associations are also very knowledgeable in these matters and prepared to advise and assist in the work. The most flourishing species in the surrounding district should be noted and strong, vigorous samples of those chosen should be collected for transplanting. The plants which are intended for the edges and shallows of the lake can be set by hand. These are the plants which will later provide shelter and harbour for fish fry. Transplanting in the deeper waters, up to a depth of eight feet is usually effected by tying the root to a stone and sinking it at the selected spot. Plants will not generally grow at a depth greater than eight feet because they are dependent upon light for their metabolism. After transplanting it is probable that many other plant species will appear very quickly and it may be necessary to remove some that are likely to get out of hand or conflict with the intended use of the water.

A few of the most suitable and commonly occurring aquatic and verge plants are listed below; there are many more species available in every part of the country.

Curled Pondweed (*Potamogeton crispus*)   This plant will grow in depths up to three feet without producing an excessive amount of decaying matter.

Mares Tail (*Hippuris vulgaris*)   This is a valuable aerator and it will grow in depths of up to eight feet.

Water Crowfoot (*Ranunculus Aquatilis*)   A plant that generally does very well in ponds and shallow waters.

Starworts (*Callitreche*)   These grow at medium depths.

Water Dropwort (*Oenanthe fistulosa*)   Grows close to the bank in moving water.

Arrowheads (*Sagittaria*)   These grow at shallow and medium depths providing both food and shelter to fish and to the creatures upon which fish live. They are also good oxygenators.

Water Mint (*Mentha aquatica*)   This is a perennial with creeping rootstock that grows around the edges.

Milfoils (*Myriophyllum*)   These thrive in shallow waters where they provide cover for spawn, elvers and fry. Growth may have to be kept in check.

Water Whorl Grass (*Catabrosa aquatica*)   This is a most attrac-

170

tive perennial grass of wide distribution which grows in shallow waters and on wet banks. Water fowl are fond of the young leaves.

Marsh Marigold (*Caltha palustris*) A perennial plant with conspicuous golden-coloured flowers, large glossy leaves and a thick creeping rootstock. It is also known as King Cup and Luckan Gowan and it gives a decorative touch to verges.

Floating Club Rush (*Scirpus fluitans*) A grass-like plant of wide distribution. It grows partly floating and partly above water and the plants often form dense masses at the margins.

Marsh Club Rush (*Scirpus paustris*) A plant of wide distribution which grows around the edges of lakes and ponds and on marshy banks. It has a vigorous and well-spread rootstock which sends up dense tufts of stems terminating in a red-brown spikelet.

Common Bulrush (*Scirpus lacustris*) Another marginal plant of wide distribution. The thick rootstock is creeping and perennial and it sends up tall stout stems to a height of four to eight feet according to the depth of water. Used for thatching, mat manufacture, etc.

Hortwort (*Ceratophyllum demersum*) This plant floats on the surface for most of the year, rising in the early spring and sinking to the bottom in the winter. Can be troublesome if not kept in check.

Yellow Water Lily (*Nuphar luteum*) This is an attractive plant which floats on ponds, lakes and sluggish waters. It has a thick fleshy rootstock which creeps in the mud and thick leathery heart-shaped floating leaves.

Yellow Flag (*Iris pseudacorus*) An attractive marginal plant which has a thick horizontal creeping rootstock with numerous fibres. The stem rises to a height of two feet with pale green erect leaves and bright yellow flowers.

Purple Loosestrife (*Lythrum salicaria*) A marginal plant that has a perennial creeping rootstock from which rise annual stems with spikes of purple flowers.

Great Panicled Sedge (*Carex paniculata*) The sedges are common and widely distributed marginal plants. This is a hardy

171

species which forms large tussocks with a mass of strong roots which are valuable for consolidating loose soil.

Some species are undesirable, particularly if they tend to choke the waters. Such plants should be avoided and if they obtain a hold they may have to be cleared frequently. The Floating Fern Weed or Fairy Moss (*Azolla caroliniana*) and Water Thyme or Canadian Weed (*Elodia canadensis*) are typical examples.

ANIMAL AND INSECT LIFE

At the same time as plant life is brought to the reclaimed pit, it can be stocked with some of the creatures upon which fish prey. They can be taken from any lakes, ponds, canals or other waters in the vicinity and they will multiply rapidly. These creatures cover a very wide range of life and include all the numerous snails; freshwater shrimps; plankton; daphnia or water-flea; the larvae of caddis, mayfly, yellow uprights, stoneflies, olives and duns, black gnats, willow flies; water or whirligig beetles; water boatmen; bloodworms; midge larvae; water lice; crayfish; minnows and bullhead.

The wet workings will have contained some of this animal and insect life almost as soon as they started and by the time the workings are exhausted there will probably be a sizeable population of some species, but it is still desirable to introduce a wide range before stocking with fish. If the fish food is built up in this way there is little danger of finding stunted fish later.

Fish Stocking

The time soon comes when life is well established in the new waters and they can be stocked with fish. If it is known that any angling club intends to fish the water it is advisable to enlist their services from the onset for they will then choose the fish they require and probably undertake the stocking. Generally, the large pits, exceeding thirty acres should only be developed as coarse fisheries.

The fish will probably be netted and brought from the nearest and most convenient well-stocked waters that may be available, which may be a lake, pond or reservoir. Where taken from an overstocked source the fish may appear to be small due to an inadequate food supply. Removal of the fish under such circumstances improves conditions in the original water and it is probable that the fish will grow rapidly if the food supply is abundant in the new water. It is of considerable advantage if the general conditions in the new water are similar to those prevailing in the original water. When the fish are netted and taken from their original water they should be placed in covered tanks or cans full of water and transported as quickly as possible to the new water. Only the best and healthiest-looking fish should be placed in the tanks. The fish should be handled as carefully and as little as possible so that the natural mucus is not rubbed off their bodies. For the same reason the containers should not be too crowded. On arrival at the new water the containers should be submerged and then opened for the fish to escape or the stock fish should be put into the water very carefully and gently; certainly they should not be thrown or tipped into the new water, as this would be very likely to cause injuries.

For stocking new waters, angling clubs often favour Bream, Roach and Tench, particularly if the waters are quiet and there is plenty of weed growth. Perch are frequently chosen for the deeper waters. Rudd and Gudgeon seem to do well almost anywhere and Carp prefer the smaller pool and quiet conditions. Sporting fishermen will probably wish to introduce a few Pike. If there is a flow through the workings and they are fed by springs, it may be feasible to stock Chub, Dace and Barbel. Fly-fishing is perhaps rare but not unknown in the smaller reclaimed workings. A 'game' or trout fishery calls for rather special conditions and a bio-chemical examination of the water is essential. The size of the pit might vary from one to six acres and it should be shaded so that the water temperature does not rise above 70° Fahrenheit in summer, on the other hand, there must not be too heavy a leaf fall into the water from surrounding vegetation as this increases acidity. Where the report of the bio-chemical examination is favourable and the waters are suitable they can be stocked with eyed ova purchased commercially. At somewhat greater cost they can be stocked more positively and satisfactorily with unfed fry. Where the cost is subsidiary to quick results, yearlings or takeable fish can be stocked.

Part Three

CONCLUSION

CHAPTER 12

Reclamation—A Community Task

The National Concept

It will be appreciated that there is infinite variety in dereliction problems and ample scope for ingenuity in solving them. Almost every scheme throws up some fresh local difficulty which calls for a different approach but these can be classified as tactical exercises and by and large, the equipment and experience are available to overcome all obstacles. However, there is the larger national concept and this must have regard for the extent and distribution of dereliction problems throughout the country and the strategic policy which should be pursued to resolve them on a national scale once and for all.

The estimate of 150,000 acres given in *New Life for Dead Lands*, was an attempt to measure the backlog which has accumulated during the last century. Taking into consideration (*a*) the vastly increased output and demands of the extractive industries (*b*) the greater productivity of manufacturing industries and (*c*) the extensive areas which have been programmed in development plans for mineral workings and industrial developments throughout the country, it seems that there may well be more dereliction within the next twenty or thirty years than has accumulated during the past century. However, owing to planning control and the conditions likely to be imposed in planning consents, a much smaller proportion of industrial land should remain derelict than was customary in the past. In future the operator or developer will be required to carry out some

M 177

measure of restoration or to apply some amenity treatment, as soon as working ceases, as a condition of the planning permission which he had to obtain before he started working. But it is not always practicable before development commences, to impose conditions which will ensure complete ultimate restoration and there will probably be a substantial increase in the acreage of unfilled (and from the economic standpoint—unfillable) pits. Buildings and industrial installations are still likely to be abandoned and even whole settlements may become derelict owing to movements of population. These may be movements arising from economic causes, from changes in industrial demands or from the exhaustion of mineral reserves, such as the closure of the tin plate works in South Wales or the decay of Durham villages as coal seams are worked out.

Nor is it generally practicable to prevent the continued surface tipping of spoil and wastes by the use of planning powers. In coalmining alone, some 40 million tons of 'dirt' are tipped each year, involving an annual consumption of twenty to twenty-five acres of land for each thousand workers in the industry and as far as we can see this will continue indefinitely unless underground stowage becomes the prevailing policy. Moreover, in some circumstances the damaging effects of mining subsidence cannot be prevented. All the causes of past dereliction are with us still and although the total effect will be mitigated by planning control wherever this is appropriate, some increase in the total amount of dereliction is bound to take place every year.

Who Shall Pay?

Land conservation must always be an important component of national policy in our relatively small island with its intense competition between so many land uses. Reclamation is an essential feature of land conservation, which frequently entails a net financial loss. When it does, the crucial question is always, who should foot the bill?

Prima facie, it would seem that the operator should pay (as happens in cases of compliance with the conditions of planning consents), but we have come to realize that this is frequently impracticable, particularly in respect of old dereliction which was brought about by the activities of the operator's predecessor. Again, there may be physical limitations, such as, a lack of filling material within a reasonable distance to restore an excavation. In some cases it must be acknowledged too, that the impact of restoration costs upon the economy of an industry may be so disproportionate to existing cost levels as to render their imposition infeasible. But, in this connection, it should be noted that in recent years, coal-mining subsidence has been the subject of legislation which has placed the whole future costs of making good any damage upon the National Coal Board. Of course, there still can be insuperable difficulties in establishing a claim notwithstanding this Statutory provision.

Henceforth it can be reasonably assumed that when planning permission is given for mineral workings or industrial undertakings, conditions will be imposed requiring restoration as far as it would be an equitable charge upon the operator. This circumstance should be much more acceptable to an operator than the uncertainties which prevailed in the past, especially if he knows from the development plan the after-use of the land. The operator can then plan restoration in conjunction with extraction, so that the two operations become merged in a continuous process, which can make both immensely cheaper. Furthermore, he may also be in a position to programme his working and the subsequent restoration within the years of greatest output in order to obtain maximum tax rebates. Or, if he prefers it, as he knows the term of working, he can set up a sinking fund which builds up in the most prosperous years to meet his commitments during the running-down period.

From time to time, there have been suggestions that each industry should pay by means of a general levy based upon tonnage or cubic yardage, similar to the levy placed on the Ironstone industry by the Mineral Workings Act 1951. This, however, would be unnecessary, to the extent that the costs of complying with planning conditions for restoration and landscaping will normally fall, in any case, upon the developers concerned.

In addition, there would be considerable administrative difficulties where the industries consisted of a large number of small operators. Difficulties could also be envisaged within an industry which has widely varying physical conditions to contend with, with the result that some individual workings may involve complicated and expensive reclamation works, whereas others would require comparatively little restoration. However, given good will on each side, it should be possible to negotiate—possibly without any levies—equitable restoration schemes for all extractive industries, which would be more satisfactory than the circumstances now obtaining.

Most of the reclamation which has been accomplished in the past has been undertaken by local authorities and the rate funds have borne the costs, with the aid of rate deficiency grants and sometimes with other grants for special purposes. Perhaps this is in accordance with the democratic doctrine that local authorities are responsible for the well-being of their districts and therefore should carry out at the expense of the inhabitants at large, all beneficial work which is unremunerative and which no one else will undertake. Where reclamation has been carried out by local authorities, it has usually been done as a side issue in the performance of a statutory function such as the provision of sites for housing purposes or playing fields, but there are a number of instances of reclamation having been undertaken solely for the improvement of neighbourhood amenity or the removal of an unsightly feature. Where it has been undertaken for the development of an industrial estate, the local authority can normally recoup the costs, in the selling price of the land or the terms of the lease.

Unfortunately, the incidence of dereliction is frequently heaviest in small industrial districts which have suffered a decline in their prosperity owing to exhaustion of the mineral reserves, such as Dawley in Shropshire, Coseley and Amblecote in Staffordshire, Dalton and Ince-in-Makerfield in Lancashire. These are districts which have experienced industrial closures and migration of the workers, consequently they are quite unable to support the financial burdens which reclamation of their widespread dereliction would impose upon them. Furthermore, of the 126,700 acres returned as derelict in 1955 by local planning authorities through the country, the surprising large amount of 54,000 acres was located in rural districts where the product of a penny rate is low and where the staff is small. When a district has severe dereliction and a low rateable value, not only does reclamation work become financially impossible, there are also the accompanying disabilities that the environment repels new industry, prosperity departs, the people lose hope and the place slowly sinks. There are in England, Wales and Scotland many of these places which were at one time mainsprings of industrial success and sources of the national wealth. Today they are blighted and crippled by the creeping paralysis of dereliction and unable to break the vicious circle of depression. If they had been reduced to a low state by a sudden catastrophe—by flood, fire, earthquake, famine or pestilence—the chances are that relief funds would be oversubscribed (as they were at Lynmouth) and overwhelming help would be forthcoming. It seems a curious paradox, that a nation which can be so quick and generous in opening its purse-strings for charity to the afflicted of every nation, should be so hesitant, apathetic and almost resistant to suggestions for helping its own districts and its own land, where these have been damaged in contributing to the national prosperity.

Local Land Acquisition Problems

Local authorities are often inhibited by complications and difficulties in acquiring derelict land and there is an understandable reluctance to undertake reclamation work or to plant trees upon any land which does not belong to the local authority. When authorities seek to purchase the land by agreement, they frequently find the owner both unwilling to sell and unwilling or unable to embark upon an improvement scheme himself. At the same time, local authorities are generally reluctant to use compulsory purchase powers solely for the purposes of reclamation. Moreover, where powers of compulsory acquisition are resorted to, they may be exercised in pursuance of a purpose such as housing, education or the provision of playing fields and achieve reclamation as a side issue. For this, the authorities have to be clear about the after-use of the site before any proceedings are commenced.

Even where there is a willing seller it is remarkable how often and how quickly, erstwhile waste land acquires high development values as soon as local authorities appear as potential purchasers. Valuation is frequently affected by the value of adjoining land uses and this always has greater significance than the condition of the site even when the adjoining uses will not extend over the reclaimed land. It would seem equitable so far as is practicable within current arrangements to offset the market value of derelict land by a price adjustment related to the costs of the reclamation work necessary to fit the site for its new use. Where the new use is non-remunerative, as for instance, where a public open space is proposed, local authorities find present market values of land prohibitive, especially when the adjoining uses may be industrial or residential.

Many other difficulties arise from the fact that the first steps to acquire the land generally have to be taken some years before reclamation works can proceed. During that time there can be inflationary changes in the values of waste material and land or amendments of legislation affecting land values or variations in rates of interest, any or all of which may completely falsify estimates and alter the financial incidence of a scheme.

To tackle all these problems it is very desirable that professional staff qualified and experienced in land acquisition should carry out negotiations and that they should undertake any subsequent estate management but it appears that so far only the largest local authorities have felt able to afford such staff. Where a small county district has such problems the local planning authority normally arranges assistance. It can be confidently asserted that land acquisition is almost always a much greater obstacle to reclamation than any technical problems thrown up by the work itself.

Sites Apparently Abandoned

There are some derelict sites which the owners wish to remain in a derelict condition. These sites appear to be abandoned and disused and they are always unsightly but when a local authority makes inquiries with a view to purchase and reclamation they find the owner's interest very much alive. In such cases the local authority generally retires and the site remains a nuisance to the public at large. The owner may well have a good reason—he may have temporarily abandoned the works and have genuine intentions to re-open them. This is particularly applicable to old china-clay pits and lead mines where the operators frequently submit that they may have occasion to return when commodity prices improve and justify working the pits to a greater depth.

Even in such cases where it can be accepted that works are temporarily abandoned and left in indefinite suspense, it would seem feasible and reasonable to require some measure of landscaping to be undertaken so as to reduce the unpleasant visual impact over the years which intervene before work may start again. Any such interim landscaping could be quite a cheap scheme because it would be expendable when workings recommenced. Alternatively, local authorities may have some justification for adopting a policy of acquiring for reclamation purposes, any workings or derelict sites which appear to have been abandoned, or which have ceased active operation for ten years or more. The important thing is perhaps to fix a term of years beyond which unsightly features must be treated or can be acquired for treatment.

Another similar problem is the derelict site in private ownership and used periodically as a rubbish and waste tip. The owner may collect a payment for each load tipped or he may let portions of the site for short periods as a contractor's shoot for spoil and debris. It can be the source of quite a good income, in fact, some deep pits located near large built-up areas are reputed to be earning more as waste shoots then they did during working of the mineral. Sometimes the filling of these pits is carried out in a most haphazard and piecemeal fashion and takes a very long time. At the prevailing rate of tipping these tipping sites can remain a public nuisance far too long. Little can be done in the average case beyond general tidying up and abatement of any statutory nuisance; this may entail long drawn-out and repeated legal proceedings. There are cases of large flooded marl-holes where tipping is continuous, but they are unlikely to be reclaimed for a century at the present tipping rate and it would seem reasonable for local authorities to take steps to ensure satisfactory reclamation of these potential danger spots within a limited number of years.

Use of derelict land for tipping can give rise to other local difficulties, as for example, when adjoining derelict sites are in different ownerships and the dumping of rubbish is taking place upon them at varying levels. The results can be more unsightly and offensive than the original dereliction and unless steps are taken by the local authority to co-ordinate tipping activities on such sites the conditions go from bad to worse. It merely requires co-ordination to ensure that reclamation shall be achieved instead of further devastation.

In the clearance of burnt shale tips there is again a distinct possibility of the last state being worse than the former state. This happens when a contractor quarries the spoilheap for good metalling and hard burnt shale, leaving the inferior material and dust (which perhaps forms half the original bulk) in more disarray and with much more harsh and jagged outlines than the original heap.

Training for the Services

In particular circumstances, it may be practicable for local authorities engaged on reclamation work to make arrangements to employ various agencies for clearing derelict land. The clearance and rehabilitation of very large and difficult sites could provide valuable practical training for Royal Engineer units (both Regular and Territorial) in the handling and use of heavy mechanical equipment and in the calculation, fixing and

Plate 43. Trees planted on spoilheap at Littleburn near Durham becoming established

Plate 44 (a and b). A good example of the screening of industrial plant

Plate 45. Well screened gravel workings showing the tree screen in the background and an island left for wildfowl in foreground

Plate 46. Chasewater, reclaimed as a water sports area. The adjoining recreational area was filled and levelled with pulverized fuel ash from the Rugeley electricity generating station.

Plate 47. An old gravel pit at Dorchester-on-Thames, Oxfordshire, which has received amenity treatment. A shelving shingle-beach has been made; old offices were converted into a club house; slipways, jetties, moorings and other sailing facilities were constructed

Plate 48. Mining subsidence at Kimblesworth, Co. Durham. Houses in foreground demolished. Houses in background shored up.

firing of demolition charges. Airfield Construction Groups of the Royal Air Force could find similar wide scope for training with earth-moving plant in the levelling and restoration of mineral workings. There are many areas, which for one reason or another are unlikely to be dealt with by local authorities and Service units might undertake their rehabilitation with advantage to the units and to the general public. They could for instance be particularly useful in dealing with abandoned Royal Ordnance Factory sites and obsolete defence works of all sorts. Apparently trade union objections and insurance difficulties can only be reconciled at high level, but power to sanction and implement any reclamation scheme should be available at Command rather than War Office level. Command Training Officers might even be urged to seek such potential training areas particularly as an Engineer Regiment costs more than £10,000 a week to train and maintain.

Poor agricultural land in remote situations has generally had to be chosen for training areas (occasionally in a National Park or Nature Reserve) and hills and hollows have had to be constructed for armoured vehicle training grounds. When the site is remote, heavy transport demands are involved for moving units to and from their stations which are generally in or near populous areas. Derelict sites on the other hand can usually be found within or close to urban areas and they are relatively easily accessible; many have the hills and hollows already formed. An abandoned large industrial site covering perhaps 200 acres or more, may contain tall chimney stacks, massive concrete foundations for plant and machinery, reinforced concrete structures, blast furnaces, retorts, railway sidings, canal basins, dilapidated buildings, slag heaps or deep excavations. Such a site can entail a most complicated and expensive clearance task for a local authority even when the authority engages demolition contractors, but it is exactly the sort of site which affords excellent and varied opportunities when exploited as a Services training ground before being put to its new uses.

Conclusion

Contribution of the Universities

Many other agencies can become involved in tackling the problems of dereliction, and for this purpose, information and assistance may be sought by local authorities from a variety of sources. During the last ten years an increasing interest has been apparent in the Universities and a remarkably wide range of studies appertaining to the problems is being built up. At the onset, reclamation became a popular subject for theses and from there it has advanced to become a team-project for staff and students in many disciplines with the object of examining and assessing the impact of local dereliction and the possibilities of overcoming it as a planned operation.

In August 1961 the University of Swansea in conjunction with the local authority, the Department of Scientific and Industrial Research and industrialists, began a detailed study into the causes and effects of dereliction in the lower valley of the River Tawe at Landore where 1,200 acres are derelict. A hundred years ago this site was filled with active heavy industry; today its giant spoilheaps and ruinous factories present a desolate landscape which extends to within half a mile of the town centre of Swansea. Six University Departments are already involved in the survey and the cost is met from grants made by the Nuffield Foundation and others. Physical studies are being made by the Departments of Civil Engineering, Geology, Geography and Botany and social studies are being carried out by the Departments of Social Administration and Economics. The Lower Swansea Valley Project, as the survey is called, will involve soil surveys, geological surveys, traffic studies and studies of industrial growth, housing and open space. The University will contribute the research skills and computer programmes while the local authority will contribute local knowledge and statutory powers. This intensive investigation into the needs of the area will be followed by preparation of a reclamation project providing good living conditions and adequate communications. When the study is completed and proposals are prepared it is

186

intended that the scheme shall be included in the development plan review of the County Borough.

The Department of Architecture (Planning Research Unit) of the University of Edinburgh is co-operating with the Department of Social and Economic Research of the University of Glasgow in the preparation of a survey and plan for Mid Lothian and West Lothian which has similar objectives in the rehabilitation of worked-out areas and the improvement of living conditions within the region. This Regional Plan covers an area of some eighty-four square miles of the lowlands between Glasgow and Edinburgh which has been intensively mined for coal, oil shales and clay. At present the district harbours extensive dereliction and is subject to subsidence while the whole countryside is dominated by huge bings and wasteheaps. Redemption of the Lothians will be one of the finest civic achievements of Scotland and a new town will be provided in the process.

Many other Universities have massive dereliction almost on their doorsteps and it can be reasonably anticipated that eventually most of them will follow these pioneering examples.

Other Agencies

There is unlimited scope too for participation by voluntary organizations and local societies, particularly those associated with youth movements, in the transformation of innumerable small derelict sites into amenity features. Scattered throughout the countryside are odd 'borrow pits', small quarries, sand pits and minor tips which are rarely taken into account in derelict land surveys. Some may be so placed, that their treatment is desirable in the public interest. These sites need not be levelled or subjected to expensive treatment; frequently they only require cleaning up and a little planting so that they can form timbered hillocks or dales and thus serve as landscape features instead of being eyesores.

There is the added advantage that those persons who partake in such voluntary schemes, subsequently value and tend to protect the feature quite effectively. Far too often when local

187

authorities carry out improvement schemes, particularly tree planting schemes, they suffer from vandalism. And the vandals can be the very same persons who would have conserved the feature had they helped to create it. If we can foster the creative spirit, the destructive urge dies away. This makes the work so eminently suitable for youth organizations, student work camps and similar activities.

Overspill

In the context of regional and national planning another facet of derelict land emerges—its suitability for the accommodation of overspill from the conurbations. In the heart of the Black Country, there are many districts with a high proportion of derelict land and they have long been regarded as reception areas, on redevelopment, for overspill population and industry from other more congested parts of the West Midlands conurbation. The publication *Conurbation* produced by the West Midland Group in 1948 presented the redevelopment of blighted areas and derelict land as a solution to the regional problem. This was to a great extent endorsed by the West Midland Plan produced by Abercrombie and Jackson a little later. Consequently all the development plans of the local planning authorities concerned have been influenced by these recommendations. Thus it was that derelict land in Coseley has been proposed for redevelopment for housing and industrial purposes, so that the population of the urban district could increase from 36,000 to 44,000. Similarly the population of Wednesfield was to increase from 19,000 to 36,000 and the population of the Borough of Brierley Hill was to increase from 52,000 to 62,500.

A similar opportunity for the accommodation of overspill population and industry from the West Midlands conurbation is being exploited on derelict land at Dawley and within the Coalbrookdale district of East Shropshire. In this locality over 9,000 acres have now been designated as the site for a new town to accommodate 90,000 people. The Dawley–Stirchley area was first suggested by the author as a new town site early in 1948 at a

188

meeting of the Institution of Municipal Engineers in Birmingham. A little later, following upon the West Midlands Plan of Abercrombie and Jackson, the author as Regional Planning Officer for the West Midlands, undertook an exploratory survey of the region and its immediate surroundings in search of new town sites which would be capable of relieving pressures within the conurbation. A reconnaissance of some thirty sites was made and eventually these were winnowed down to four of which Dawley was one. A detailed survey and appreciation of each of these four sites was then prepared in the Regional Office and this highlighted the advantages of reclaiming the land around Dawley.

However, the Ministry's memorandum concerning the West Midlands Plan, issued to local planning authorities in November 1950, confirmed a policy of expanding existing towns and gave population targets upon which were based all the development plans, subsequently submitted under the Town and Country Planning Act 1947, by the local planning authorities affected. Owing to the comparative failure of town expansion schemes to meet the needs of the conurbation, further consideration of Dawley as the site for a new town started in 1955. By 1960 Shropshire County Council was formally notified that Dawley was likely to be chosen as the site for a new town and this choice was endorsed by all the local authorities concerned, the Town and Country Planning Association, the New Towns Society and public opinion generally.

Manchester has encountered strong opposition to its proposals for overspill reception in Cheshire because valuable agricultural land would have to be built over. In South-East Lancashire there are some 4,000 acres of derelict land adjoining over 8,000 acres of low quality agricultural land within the borough of Leigh and the urban districts of Abram, Aspall, Atherton, Hindley, Ince and Tydlesley. In these districts the existing built-up areas cover about 7,000 acres and they accommodate a population of about 140,000. *Prima facie*, it would seem that Manchester's overspill could be taken by these towns and this would probably result in stronger administrative units and improved social facilities. However, a great deal of reclamation would probably have to be done before these areas become attractive to Manchester.

These examples demonstrate that large blocks of dereliction proffer magnificent opportunities and wherever they occur the possibilities should be considered, of accommodating overspill population and industry from overcrowded conurbations, by the promotion of comprehensive schemes under the New Towns Act 1946 or the Town Development Act 1952.

Mining Subsidence and Stowage

Mining subsidence damages all types of buildings, roads, bridges, railways, gas and water mains, sewers and every form of construction. The land itself is also damaged, drainage is disrupted and 'flashes' and flooded areas are produced. Whatever the cost may be in compensation, this covers only a fraction of the loss and damage which is caused by mining subsidence. (See Plate 48).

There is a dread of subsidence in all mining areas as was recently illustrated at Coventry when the National Coal Board announced that an extension of the colliery workings was necessary to win the coal beneath the city—estimated to be something of the order of 100 million tons. Immediately there was widespread opposition from all the commercial, industrial and civic interests. The industrialized northern half of the city would be affected by the proposal and the City Council formally objected on behalf of the many interests likely to be affected because heavy subsidence damage was feared notwithstanding reassurances from the National Coal Board. In the public interest the Board offered to restrict workings by adopting a partial extraction system and leaving extensive pillars of support which would entail sacrifice of an asset worth over £200 million at present coal values.

Numerous instances have occurred where long-abandoned underground workings have had to be filled by local authorities at the public expense owing to their potential danger or because building or constructional work was being undertaken on the surface. When the Sheffield College of Technology was built in 1957 major infilling works had to be carried out in order to secure the foundations. Darlaston Urban District Council had to fill undermined land at Catharine's Cross in 1963 before they could proceed with a scheme to provide housing accommodation and shops. As is often the case, the cavitation was only discovered when the foundation trench for the first block of flats collapsed.

Recently at Dudley, some old limestone underground workings partially collapsed and threatened a housing site, bus garage and the main radial road, The remedial work of backfilling with sand was estimated to cost the borough council at least £70,000, and this will only deal with a small part of extensive workings. Further subsidence may occur in adjoining workings. The costs of filling the first portion is probably greater than the total profits which accrued from the original extraction of the limestone.

In all these cases, surveying of the cavities is often dangerous and the necessary exploration work, borings, hydraulic sand stowage and pressure grouting is expensive—much more dangerous and costly than it would have been, had the backfilling been carried out immediately mining ceased and before the works were abandoned. When trouble is met today, it is usually due to mining operations during the eighteenth and early nineteenth centuries, when mining was on a comparatively small scale. There are few records of these old workings and when they are suspected beneath a building site, every effort should be made to obtain an old mine working plan. If a record is available, its accuracy may be verified by a few borings, otherwise it may be necessary to consider the sinking of an exploratory shaft. As time goes on the amount of cavitation to be remedied is likely to increase because the scale of mining operations has vastly expanded. However, mining records of operations since 1872 are available and with these and the information contained in geological maps it is generally possible to build up a fairly reliable picture of the subterranean conditions.

Conclusion

Almost all subsidence problems would be obviated if under-ground back-stowage was universally required to be carried out before abandonment of mine workings. This stowage could make good use of much of the material now put into spoilheaps and so remedy, or at least ameliorate two nuisances at the same time. Working would then be programmed so that packing of mine waste, grouting and sealing takes place as headings and drifts are exhausted. After mechanical packing with waste, a grout with only a slightly cementatious quality would seem sufficient to pump into the abandoned workings and pulverized fuel ash slurry appears to be ideal for this purpose. Up to the present, stowage has been little used in this country, although it has been widely adopted on the Continent. Where existing workings are not adapted to stowage there may be good reasons for not adopting the practice and in general it is necessary to weigh these reasons and the expense involved, against the need and advantages of maintaining the ground surface at its normal level. Cost is invariably quoted as the deterrent reason but it must be questionable whether the cost of back-stowage is greater than the ultimate costs of neglect to deal with the subsidence problem satisfactorily and permanently. Temporarily it may be cheaper—as it undoubtedly was to the entrepreneur who exploited the Dudley limestone.

Cost has always been held as the deterrent to every social improvement. It was cost which held up public water supplies and sewerage for centuries until the Public Health Act of 1875. Cost made the provision of municipal housing impossible until the public conscience determined to abolish slums in 1909; since then, abolition of the slums and rehousing has been the main theme of every political party. It was cost that made smoke abatement impracticable until the Clean Air Act of 1956 and there are plenty of other similar instances. It is inconceivable that in this atomic age, human ingenuity should be unable to devise a technique and methods which will make stowage in appropriate cases a positive cure for subsidence and one which is attainable at reasonable cost.

Bibliography

Ministry of Town and Country Planning, *Report on the Restoration in the Ironstone Industry of the Midlands* (The Waters Report), H.M.S.O. 1946.

Oxenham, J. R., 'The Reclamation of Derelict Land,' *Journal*, Institution of Municipal Engineers, Volume 75, No. 3, 1948.

Ministry of Town and Country Planning, *Report of the Advisory Committee on Land and Gravel* (Waters Committee), H.M.S.O. 1948–1953.

Whyte, R. O., and Sisam, J. W. B., 'The Establishment of Vegetation on Industrial Waste Land,' Commonwealth Agricultural Bureaux Joint Publication No. 14, 1949.

Beaver, S. H., 'Surface Minerals in Relation to Planning,' *Report of Town and Country Planning Summer School*, 1949.

Stamp, L. Dudley, 'The Reclamation of Abandoned Industrial Areas,' *Journal*, Royal Society of Arts, 1951.

Russell, Sir E. J., 'Rehabilitation of Devastated Areas,' *Journal*, British Association for the Advancement of Science, Volume 7, 1951.

Oxenham, J. R., *The Restoration of Derelict Land*, Report of Public Works and Municipal Services Congress, 1952.

Hadfield, C. N., 'The Restoration of Derelict Land following Mineral Extraction,' *Journal*, Royal Institute of Chartered Surveyors, Volume 32, 1952.

Rees, W. J., and Skelding, A. D., 'Grass Establishment on Power Station Waste,' *Agriculture*, Volume 59, 1953.

Town Planning Institute, Research Committee, 'Problems of Land Restoration after Surface Mineral Workings,' 1954.

Bates, A., 'Site Reclamation in Practice,' *Journal*, Town Planning Institute, Volume 40, 1954.

Bibliography

Beaver, S. H., 'Land Reclamation after Surface Mineral Working,' *Journal*, Town Planning Institute, Volume 41, 1955.

Ministry of Housing and Local Government, Circular 9/55, *First Review of Development Plans*, H.M.S.O. 1955.

Wood, R. F., and Thirgood, J. V., 'Tree Planting on Colliery Spoil Heaps,' Forestry Commission Research Paper No. 17, 1955.

Ministry of Housing and Local Government, Technical Memorandum No. 3, *Mineral Working*, 1955.

Browne, K., 'Dereliction,' *Architectural Review*, Volumes 118 and 119, 1955 and 1956.

Ministry of Housing and Local Government, Technical Memorandum No. 7, 'Derelict Land and its Reclamation,' 1956.

Coates, U. A., 'New Land for Old.' County Councils' Association Gazette, 1957.

Bates, A., 'The Rehabilitation of Mine and Industrial Waste Heaps,' *Planning Outlook*, Volume 4, 1957.

Ministry of Housing and Local Government, Technical Memorandum. 'Pulverised Fuel Ash,' 1958.

Wibberley, G. P., *Agriculture and Urban Growth*, Joseph, 1959.

Ministry of Housing and Local Government, Circular 26/59, *Colliery Spoil Heaps*, H.M.S.O. 1959.

Gravel Pits and Agriculture (and pamphlets relating to Building, Nature, Recreation and Water Sports), Sand and Gravel Association, 1959–1963.

Casson, J., 'Landscape Conservation,' *Planning Outlook*, Volume 5, 1959.

Ministry of Housing and Local Government, Circular 30/60. *Rehabilitation of Derelict, Neglected or Unsightly Land*, H.M.S.O. 1960.

Hartwright, T. U., 'Planting Trees and Shrubs in Gravel Workings,' Sand and Gravel Association, 1960.

Ministry of Housing and Local Government, *The Control of Mineral Working*, H.M.S.O. 1960.

Beaver, S. H., 'Land Reclamation,' *Journal*, Royal Institute of Chartered Surveyors, Volume 92, 1960.

Davies, W. Morley, 'Land Restoration following Mineral Extraction and Deposition of Waste Materials,' *Journal*, Royal Agricultural Society, Volume 122, 1961.

Central Electricity Generating Board, 'Agricultural Value of Pulverised Fuel Ash,' 1961.

Ministry of Housing and Local Government, *Report of Technical Committee on Pollution of Water by Tipped Refuse*, H.M.S.O. 1961.

Graham, M., and Butler, B., 'Play Sward on Colliery Shale,' *Town and Country Planning*, Volume 30, 1962.

Ministry of Agriculture, Fisheries and Food, Advisory Leaflet 510, *Farming Restored Opencast Land*, H.M.S.O. 1962.

Ministry of Agriculture, Fisheries and Food, *Experimental Husbandry*, No. 7, H.M.S.O. 1962.

Hackett, B., 'The Landscape of Waste,' *Landscape Architecture*, Volume 52, 1962.

Atkinson, J. R., 'The Industrial Landscape,' *Journal*, Town Planning Institute, Volume 49, 1963.

Ministry of Housing and Local Government, *New Life for Dead Lands*, H.M.S.O. 1963.

Ministry of Housing and Local Government, Circular No. 55/64, 'Annual Returns of Derelict Land,' 1964.

Civic Trust, *Derelict Land*, 1964.

Forestry Commission, *Forestry in Great Britain*, 1964.

IGNEOUS AND METAMORPHIC ROCKS

SAND AND GRAVEL

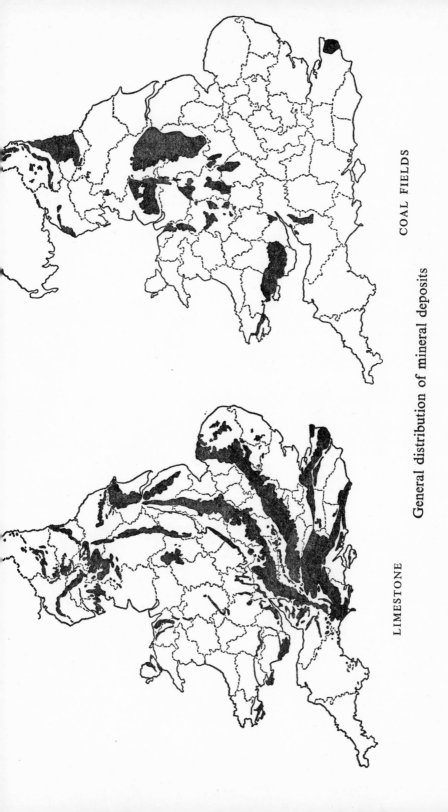

LIMESTONE

COAL FIELDS

General distribution of mineral deposits

Index

Index

Index

202